cDOWELL TECHNICAL INSTITUTE

STATE
DEPT. C ☑ **W9-CHN-575**
LIBRARIES

McDOWELL TECHNICAL INSTITUTE
LIBRARY
ACCESSION NO. 7590

The Teacher and the Law

The Teacher and the Law

Daniel Jon Gatti
and
Richard DeY Gatti

Parker Publishing Company, Inc.
West Nyack, New York

© 1972 *by*

PARKER PUBLISHING COMPANY, INC.

West Nyack, N.Y.

*All rights reserved. No part of this book
may be reproduced in any form or by any
means, without permission in writing from
the publisher.*

"This publication is designed to provide accurate and
authoritative information with regard to the subject matter covered. It is sold with the understanding that the
publisher is not engaged in rendering legal, accounting, or
other professional advice. If legal advice or other expert
assistance is required, the services of a competent professional person should be sought.

*—From a Declaration of Principles jointly adopted
by a Committee of the American Bar Association
and a Committee of Publishers and Associations.*"

Library of Congress Cataloging in Publication Data

Gatti, Daniel Jon, (Date)
   The teacher and the law.

   Includes bibliographical references.
   1. Teachers--Legal status, laws, etc.--United
States. I. Gatti, Richard DeY   joint
author. II. Title.
KF4175.Z9G3   344'.73'078   72-5192
ISBN 0-13-888073-5

Printed in the United States of America

TO OUR DAD

Foreword

Teachers are more conscious these days of such law-related matters as constitutional rights and "academic freedom." This book offers a practical view of such matters on the realistic basis of what the law is, how it affects teachers, and how it is developing. In short, a realistic portrayal of existing law is set forth, rather than an argumentative view of what the law "ought to be" from one point of view or another.

This book also analyzes legal matters of even more importance to teachers from a bread-and-butter point of view. The law of contracts affects every public school teacher, but probably rather few are aware of this area of law as it affects them in their chosen careers. The presentation of this all-encompassing subject alone makes this book a "must" for all teachers.

The law of torts as it affects teachers is another area that has not had the general attention it deserves; yet every teacher should know the basic pitfalls of "tort law" that lie in wait as traps for the unwary and the uninformed. Here is another legal subject presented which, of itself, makes the book a necessity in the hands of teachers.

Also realistically presented are vital matters of relationships with the school board, tenure, and grievance procedures, each of which is a subject that directly affects every teacher.

And finally, the book ends with a clear and down-to-earth discussion of the student-teacher relationship and "student rights" the teacher should be aware of.

While there is no substitute for the necessity of consulting an attorney when a real problem exists, this book should serve as a general guide on most legal problems that might affect a teacher. It will serve as a valuable manual that will inform teachers of the basic laws that affect them in their professional duties. It is a practical guide to action on a day-to-day basis: what a teacher should do, and what a teacher ought not to do. It is written by authors who have had both public school teaching experience and legal training.

7

In my own capacity as a professor of law at the College of Law of Willamette University, I have had frequent personal contact with the authors, and have had the pleasure of their participation in a number of courses taught by me here. On the basis of such contact, I consider the authors well qualified to write this book. I also commend the book highly for its combination of scholarship and practical approach, and am most pleased to recommend it as something that should be in the hands of every public school teacher in the United States.

Henry J. Bailey, III
Professor of Law
College of Law, Willamette University
Salem, Oregon

The Scope and Value of This Book

This book is written for public school teachers. In the primary and secondary grades, you have over two million colleagues, all working with children. You are constantly in touch with other teachers and with your administrations. You are involved. Being involved means being faced with new activities and new situations which constantly challenge even the most experienced teacher. It also means that sometime, sooner or later, you are likely to become involved with the law.

The Teacher and the Law offers practical guidelines for the protection of teachers, and for the protection of teachers' rights. As a teacher, you know that there are many legal problems with which an educator must deal. They might involve such things as whether or not to strike, an assault on a teacher in the school, or a suit brought against a teacher for negligence. It could be a situation where a teacher is being ordered to shave, or a group of teachers want to join actively in a civil rights movement. You have read, seen, and been directly or indirectly affected by these problems. And there will be more. But with a knowledge of what the law is, and the practical information contained in this book, you will be able to prevent or to solve many of the potential problems that could affect you in your role as a teacher.

The legal questions might concern your classroom, your students, or your administration. Questions will also arise concerning personal or contract rights. Although the approaches will vary, depending upon your individual personality, the age of your students, or the regulations under which you work, reliable guidelines will be found in this book. As a teacher, you have made rapid strides in having your constitutional rights defined, and you can be protected if you know which remedial procedures to follow. With this protection, you can take a practical approach to the immediate problems which in the past have involved endless delay and often resulted in obscure answers.

The outcome of any case with which you might become involved can depend upon a subtle point of fact or circumstance, but most legal encounters in the school fall into general areas. These areas will be covered in detail, not legalistically, but in the form of concise guidelines that you, the teacher, can follow.

The law protects you and your students. It does not favor any particular group. Instead, it is a yardstick by which all people are judged in their relationships with others. It attempts to be fair to everyone involved with your classroom. With this in mind, we believe that *The Teacher and the Law* will benefit you in your everyday contact with students, administrators, and the people in the community in which you teach.

Daniel Jon Gatti
Richard DeY Gatti

ACKNOWLEDGMENTS

We would like to express our appreciation for the assistance and ideas given to us by Mr. Jack Morton (Dean of Men, Oregon College of Education); Dr. Milt Baum (Director of Executive & Legal Services, Oregon State Board of Education); and Mr. Edwin Butler (Professor of Law, Willamette University).

We are also indebted to author and law professor Henry J. Bailey, III, for his valuable assistance and encouragement in the writing of this book. And finally, we want to especially thank our mother, who had to type and retype the manuscript a number of times. Her acute observations and pointed comments have proved invaluable.

Contents

The Teacher and the Law

ONE

Providing Teachers with Protection

In 1931, two male teachers entered a school building after it had been closed. Three female students accompanied the instructors, and, as a result, the teachers were dismissed from their classroom duties. Believing that their dismissal was improper, the teachers turned to the courts for reinstatement. However, because of the suspicious circumstances, and because the conduct invited criticisms of the teachers' morality, the court found that they were guilty of misconduct and upheld the discharge.

In this case, the teachers and students remained in the building without turning on any lights for 45 minutes. In the morning, the janitor discovered smoked cigarette butts and bread crumbs on the floor. No one proved that an "immoral" act had been committed. In fact, there was no evidence that an immoral act was even attempted. Nevertheless, the court ruled that a teacher should not transcend recognized standards of propriety, and said:

> We do not mean by what we have said to prescribe a rule of conduct measuring up to the notions of the self-constituted moralist, nor to require the teacher to abstain from every act that is proscribed by blue law advocates, but we do say that, when he engages in conduct that in the minds of a prudent and cautious person would arouse suspicions of immorality, he is then guilty of such misconduct as is contemplated by [state law].[1]

(An explanation of the cites in this text is included in the appendix.)

This decision was probably correct in its final outcome, even though the courts of today will take other things into consideration when upholding a teacher's dismissal for immorality. One must be careful that his conduct does not substantially affect his classroom rapport or performance in an adverse manner. Rapport and performance are important, but all detractions from these standards will not be a teacher's responsibility. When this is the case, however, the teacher should be prepared to follow the proper procedures in alleviating the situation.

The above case serves as a good example of a dismissal that could have been prevented. There are many times when the student-teacher relationship is charged with such emotion that you must be as delicate and tactful as possible. For example, students frequently seem to develop "crushes" on their teachers. How should you handle such a situation at the elementary or secondary levels? What can happen if you do not handle it properly?

Student crushes can generally be handled with mere common sense, but there are guidelines that should be taken into consideration. An adolescent's emotions must be respected. They are important, and must be handled *tactfully*. After a student crush can no longer be ignored, you should:

1. Never be alone with the student, if at all possible. If you cannot avoid being alone with him or her, keep the doors open, or find a more suitable place for whatever is being discussed.
2. Discuss the problem with an adult figure within the school, a person whom the student respects. If possible, this person should have a frank and open discussion with the student, explaining the impossibilities of such a relationship.
3. If suggestion No. 2 doesn't seem appropriate in your situation, and if the student is mature, you might carry on the discussion yourself.
4. Make certain that the student's counselor or your administration is aware of the situation. This could prevent future inquiries that might be tainted.
5. This is a private matter, and should not be made a matter of public knowledge. This means that it should be handled within the school. Doctors, parents, etc., should only be called in as a last resort.
6. Be kind, but be firm. Words with double connotations and innocent acts of flirtation should be avoided. Understanding and tact are the key words of guidance. Consultation works when coupled with honesty, and the student will benefit as a result.

If you follow this procedure in handling a student crush, you should be free from criticism, and the student will generally outgrow the emotion. If you do not follow this procedure, the student may suffer emotionally.

CHANGING LAWS AFFECT ALL TEACHERS IN OUR SCHOOLS

When you work within the school, you are an active participant in innumerable activities and learning experiences. These activities are an important element in your students' educational growth. Sometimes they also serve as a breeding ground for encounters with legal problems that affect your position or security.

The phrase "legal problems" probably connotes something to avoid. This is not necessarily true. Legal problems can generally be solved with a basic knowledge of your rights and responsibilities as a classroom teacher.

Your rights will touch the rights of your students and the school board. Guidelines can be established which tell how these rights, intermingled as they are, work together.

Because of your unique responsibility, there are a great many laws which help to facilitate your job and make it easier. There are also laws which impose certain restrictions on things you can and cannot do or say. It is not difficult to understand the law, once you familiarize yourself with how the law affects you in particular circumstances. Circumstances change, and so does the law, and the changes have generally been for the betterment of teachers.

If the law favored any particular group in the past, it was school boards over teachers, and teachers over students. Today, the law generally compromises between these groups with decisions aimed at enhancing the student's education while enabling teachers to work freely within educational objectives. The law will continue to change. However, the course of these changes can be charted with some accuracy. There is a continuing similarity between laws of different states, and most areas of educational law have stabilized to such a point that valid generalizations can be made.

GUIDE **RULE**	BEING A TEACHER MAKES YOU RESPONSIBLE FOR YOUR STUDENTS' INSTRUCTION, SUPERVISION AND SAFETY. IF YOU DO NOT FULFILL THIS RESPONSIBILITY, YOU MAY BE HELD LIABLE.

Being "held liable" means being answerable criminally or in civil damages for something you have done that is improper or wrong. Another way to express it is that you are responsible for something you ought not to have done or something you ought to have done.

Your liability as a teacher varies with the circumstances in which you are involved. Liability can be prevented where you have understood the law and acted accordingly. You should understand your legal capacity in the classroom, what areas of the law affect you daily, and when you can be saved from paying for an injury. This understanding will make your teaching job easier and your teaching career more secure.

WHAT IS THE TEACHER'S LEGAL CAPACITY IN THE CLASSROOM?

When you enter your school building, you enter into a specific legal framework. Because you are an employee of the state, you are able to enjoy many of the state's protections. You are an extension of the state arm. This means that you are not only an employee, but you are, in essence, also an "officer" of the state when you are acting within the scope of your duty towards students.

You *owe* your students instruction and supervision, and you have a duty to conduct the classroom (including the materials used) in a safe and orderly manner. If you do not instruct properly, you may be dismissed or denied renewal of your contract. If you do not supervise your students and their activities, you may be dismissed or liable for any injuries that result from this lack of supervision. If you create a dangerous situation, or permit a hazardous condition to remain in the classroom or on the playground, you may be liable for any injuries that result from your negligence, in addition to being held responsible to your school board.

The degree or the extent of your duty toward students depends upon the circumstances. In attempting to determine if you have failed in fulfilling a certain duty, you should take into consideration such things as:

1. Written school board policies;
2. Past customs and practices within the school;
3. Specific rules and regulations; and
4. What would be reasonable and prudent in the same or similar situations.

Coupled with your duties is your authority. You have the right to expect certain behavior from students. In addition to the legal relationship between you and the state, there is a legal relationship between you and your students. This relationship, for example, obligates you to act where you see that action is necessary in order to preserve safety. Moreover, you have the right to make reasonable rules which regulate your students' conduct. This legal relationship carries with it the right to enforce discipline within the school. It does not mean you can do anything you wish. Your authority is limited to that authority which is reasonable under the circumstances. This is necessary, and will be developed in depth as specific cases and situations are discussed.

WHAT AREAS OF THE LAW AFFECT TEACHERS DAILY?

There are basically three areas of law that you should understand before you step into the classroom. They are:

1. Tort liabilities of teachers and students;
2. Constitutional rights of teachers and students; and
3. Contractual rights and responsibilities of teachers and school boards.

Torts:

If one commits a crime, he has broken a law against society. If one commits a tort, he has broken a law against an individual. People have the right to be free from physical and mental injury. They have the right to be secure and feel secure in their life, liberty and property. Therefore, all people owe all other people the duty of not infringing upon these rights. If a person violates that duty, the injured party has the right to be reimbursed for any injury caused by the violation. In other words, a tort consists of four elements:

1. *Duty.* The duty to respect other people's rights.
2. *Violation.* The breaking of that duty owed to another person.
3. *Cause.* The violation of another's rights having caused injury to that person.
4. *Injury.* The person violated being injured mentally or physically.

Each of the four elements mentioned is necessary if a person is to be liable in a tort lawsuit. The first element, *duty,* is very important to understand. What is your duty in relation to your students? Once that is determined, you will be able to better understand what you can and cannot do with children under your care. You have duties that should not be violated. Students have duties that should not be violated. If there is a violation, and that violation causes an injury, liability can be imposed.

A tort can be committed intentionally. Chapter Two discusses intentional torts in depth and defines your legal duties in this area. Negligence is also a tort, and you should be aware of your duties in this area. Chapter Three gives you specific guidelines to follow in preventing negligent injury to students. By guarding against tortious injuries, you protect yourself and your students. Thus, your working conditions will be safer, and your educational objectives will be easier to realize.

Constitutional Rights:

People have always had constitutional rights. However, in the past it was felt that broad limitations could be imposed on the constitutional rights of teachers and students. Some restrictions on teachers' and students' rights are valid even today, but the law has made drastic changes from the past. The courts of today clearly hold that teachers and students do not "shed their constitutional rights at the schoolhouse gates." Subject to reasonable restrictions, you and your students have a right to free speech, in and out of the classroom, and your private life and political philosophy may form the basis for your dismissal only in very limited situations.

Contracts:

Basically, a contract is:

1. An *agreement* between two or more parties,
2. In *understandable* and *concurring* terms,

3. Which is *binding* on both sides; and
4. Which is *supported* by consideration. (For our purpose, "consideration" is something of value given or promised for some act or promise by the other person.)

In the case of a teaching contract, you agree with the school district to fulfill certain obligations, and, in turn, the district agrees to pay you for the duties performed. It is important to know that, when you sign a contract, you incur certain responsibilities, rights, and liabilities that are protected by the contract.

Contract problems can arise in cases where the terms of the agreement are not clearly expressed but are somehow implied. No contract, however elaborate, can clearly express a solution to every possible problem. When you sign a contract, you agree to teach students whatever subject, at whatever grade level, is expressly stated on the paper; but there are other obligations that both you and the school board must adhere to. You should understand and know the limits of these obligations. If either you or the school district do not do what is promised or implied, the injured party can sue for the damages caused. There are specific procedures the injured party must take; if he follows the correct line of action, many problems can easily be avoided.

UNDERSTANDING THE LIABILITY OF A TEACHER

Public sentiment is of major importance to you and your schools. The public voices a loud opinion about school matters because the schools are generally supported by the community's willingness to pay taxes. You have authority over your students because the public realizes the necessity of such authority. The public insists that their children be given an opportunity to become intelligent, responsible human beings, and that demand is placed directly upon the shoulders of learning institutions. Because the task of educating young people involves so many different variables, you are allowed to exercise a great deal of discretion in carrying out educational objectives.

Most cases which involve teacher liability include situations where the legal duty owed by the teacher to the student has not been observed. The best way to determine if such a situation exists, is to ask:

GUIDE RULE DID THE ACT WHICH CAUSED THE INJURY EXCEED REASONABLE LIMITS, TO THE POINT WHERE THE TEACHER WAS NOT ACTING WITHIN THE RIGHTS OF HIS EMPLOYMENT? IF SO, HE IS RESPONSIBLE.

For example, you cannot injure a child if all you want is attention to a lecture being given. However, if the student is threatening you with actions that would reasonably cause the ordinary teacher to be put in a state of fear for his immediate personal safety, an act in self-defense might be appropriate. Of course, this isn't recommended except in emergency situations. Generally, you should send the student to the administrator in charge of discipline.

You are liable for your own torts, but you are not liable for the torts of others unless you are somehow involved, or negligent in the act which causes the injury. If your school district has not abandoned its legal protection from being sued (governmental immunity) you will have to pay out of your own pocket all damages that can be attributed to your involvement or negligence.

Personal liability for torts is also extended to the student. For example, if a student hits another, he is liable, and generally his parents are not. This can develop into complications under certain circumstances where the school district is under the duty of supervising the children when the injury occurs. Although the parent of a child is generally not liable for this child's torts, there are times when the teacher in charge, or the school district, can be responsible along with the student.

Students are responsible for their own torts. This is significant to teachers who are involved with children each day. However, practically speaking, if a teacher is injured by a child, either intentionally or accidentally, the teacher has few ways of being compensated other than by insurance.

SAVING THE HARMLESS TEACHER

Although the layman does not hear about "governmental immunity" too often, the concept is well known in the courts and local governments across the country. In colloquial language, it means: "You can't sue city hall," and in many courts today this is still true.

Governmental immunity is an old concept stemming from the belief that "the king can do no wrong." In America, our government and governmental branches represent the traditional concept of kinghood. Through the years, we have begun to realize that the "governmental king" has at times committed injuries that should be compensated. Nevertheless, even today you cannot sue city hall unless the government gives you permission. Permission is given when the government waives its right to immunity in circumstances it deems appropriate.

There are differences as to how immunity will affect your liability within the school. These differences are dependent upon the laws of the state where you teach. Your school gets its powers from your state legislature. The school is a representative of the state when it is carrying out its role of educating children. As an agent of the state, the school becomes the state. Therefore, the school becomes the same type of king or city hall that many people have not been able to get satisfaction from in the past. However, this immunity does not always extend to the teacher. The teacher is liable for his own torts, and if he injures someone, he must pay out of his own pocket. That is, he must pay out of his own pocket unless the state in which he teaches has given school districts permission to "save" the teacher from this expense and pay the "harmless" teacher's debt. Whether the state in which you work has done this or not, and if so, to what extent, is an area that can be broken into four parts. (See Exhibit 1.)

DOCTRINE OF NON-LIABILITY AND GOVERN- MENTAL IMMUNITY	SECTION I States where the school district can- not be sued. Teacher is not protected.	SECTION II States where suit depends on whether or not the act was gov- ernmental or proprietary.	SECTION III States where suit is valid when it is for causes named in general lia- bility insur- ance policies	SECTION IV States where school districts can be held liable for the negligent acts of its teachers. Teacher is pro- tected.
ALABAMA	X			
ALASKA				X
ARIZONA				X
ARKANSAS		II*		
CALIFORNIA				X
COLORADO				X
CONNECTICUT				X
DELAWARE		X		
FLORIDA			X	
GEORGIA		X		
HAWAII				X
IDAHO				II
ILLINOIS				X
INDIANA				II
IOWA				X
KANSAS			I	
KENTUCKY	X			

EXHIBIT 1

State					
LOUISIANA		X			
MAINE	I				
MARYLAND			II		
MASSACHUSETTS				X	
MICHIGAN		X			
MINNESOTA				X	
MISSISSIPPI			I		
MISSOURI				X	
MONTANA			II		
NEBRASKA				X	
NEVADA				X	
NEW HAMPSHIRE			II		
NEW JERSEY				X	
NEW MEXICO			II		
NEW YORK				X	
NORTH CAROLINA			II		
NORTH DAKOTA			I		
OHIO		X			CHANGING ⟶
OKLAHOMA			I		CHANGING ⟶
OREGON				X	
PENNSYLVANIA		X			CHANGING ⟶
RHODE ISLAND		X			
SOUTH CAROLINA		X			
SOUTH DAKOTA	X				
TENNESSEE			I		
TEXAS		X			
UTAH				X	
VERMONT			II		
VIRGINIA			I		
WASHINGTON				X	
WEST VIRGINIA		X			
WISCONSIN				X	
WYOMING			II		

NOTE: An excellent book on this subject is *School District Tort Liability in the 70's*, Knaak, William C., Merric Publishing Co., St. Paul, Minn.

* "II"–Liability for named acts in the insurance policy. "I"–Liability of school is limited to injuries resulting from transportation accidents.

EXHIBIT 1 (cont.)

McDOWELL TECHNICAL INSTITUTE LIBRARY
MARION, NORTH CAROLINA

Non-Liability and Governmental Immunity

Category 1. Complete Immunity—The teacher cannot look to his employer for financial help. Since teachers under this view can be held liable, it is a good idea for them to carry liability insurance. Most unions and educational associations automatically insure their members.

Category 2. Governmental v. Proprietary (the word *proprietary* is explained on page 28)—Depends on whether or not the teacher's act was within the scope of his duty.

Category 3. Insured Against General Liability—If the district has general liability insurance, the teacher is protected, if his acts are covered within the insurance policy.

Category 4. Immunity Waived—The school district is the ultimate bagholder of the debt, and the teacher is protected if he was within the scope of his duty.

The law of governmental immunity is not settled, and each year the arguments for and against immunity come before the courts and legislatures. Strict immunity of the school board (Category One above) is supported by those states which feel that, because the law does not provide money to the schools in the event someone is injured, there is therefore no money from which the injured party can be compensated. Another argument is that even if money were available, since the law says that school money should be spent on schools and for school purposes, it would be illegal for the district to pay an injured party, because that is not an expenditure which would benefit the school. These arguments are weak, and the law is changing from this position to one which treats the injured party more fairly.

The reason why change is necessary can be pointed out by a Pennsylvania case in which a student was beaten by other students because he would not give them his money. Similar criminal acts had frequently occurred at the school, and the existence of the danger was well known. Nevertheless, the school officials neglected to take any precautionary measures to protect the students' safety. Even though the child was injured, and even though the school district's administration had been negligent, the district was not held liable for the negligence because of Pennsylvania laws on immunity.[2] Justice Musmanno felt that the school should be held liable when he said:

> If the defendant school district had permitted a Bengal tiger to roam the school yard ... and ... Louis Husser, Jr., had been mangled by that savage beast, I cannot believe that the Majority of this Court would say that the [school district] would not be guilty of neglect in allowing such a peril to life and limb to exist. The responsibility of holding in leash a raging mob of juvenile delinquents intent on ruinous mischief cannot be less.[3]

Had the school district been under the same laws as those states which have waived immunity (Category Four above), a different outcome would seem possible. Justice Musmanno pointed out how the law is changing:

> This injustice cannot endure forever. I am satisfied that the day will arrive, and it cannot be far off, when people will laugh at solemn decisions of the courts of law which declare that everybody is responsible for his civil wrongs at law,—everybody but the government. What is government, but an institution set up by the people to protect the people? To say that anyone injured by the government cannot sue the government is like saying that a ship built by certain individuals may transport anyone but the builders.[4]

In order to further illustrate the differences between schools which are immune to being sued and those which are not, let us take a hypothetical situation. Assume school *A* and school *B* each have areas on their grounds which need supervision because of past fights or incidents which have caused students to be injured. Teacher *A* is assigned to supervise that area at school *A*, and teacher *B* is assigned to supervise the area at school *B*. Assume that teacher *A* forgot his coat, and because it was extremely cold outside, he left the area for one minute in order to fetch warmer clothes. Teacher *B* had the same problem, but after deciding he did not like the supervising duty, he stayed away from the area for thirty minutes because he "felt like it." School *A* has not waived its immunity from being sued. School *B* has waived its immunity.

If a student were injured during *A*'s absence, *A* might be held responsible for the injury. His liability would depend on whether or not the jury felt he was unreasonable in leaving for the reason he did, and if other reasonable and prudent teachers would have done the same thing in the same or similar circumstances. If the jury decided that the teacher had acted unreasonably, and was therefore negligent, *A* would have to pay for *all* damages that were suffered by the injured student. The school in which he works would not be responsible. It is true that the boys who injured the student would also be liable, but it is unlikely that they would have any money with which to pay for the injuries. Therefore, *A* is the ultimate bagholder in a district which is immune to being sued.

On the other hand, *B* is definitely negligent, and although he was irresponsible, the school will probably be the ultimate bagholder and will have to pay for all the injuries incurred by the student. The school district has the "deeper pocket," and this pocket can be reached because the school has waived its right to immunity.

Governmental immunity can be a harsh rule in many situations. Some arguments against governmental immunity have already been discussed, and there are many courts which have overruled the doctrine to various extents because it is unreasonable and irrational not to hold the government liable where its irresponsibility has caused someone to suffer. Complete immunity is not fair to the general public, and many times it causes undue hardship upon individual teachers. England and Canada have waived their right to governmental immunity, and many states, including Washington, which never has recognized the right, are either in Category Four or are moving in that direction.

The chart in Exhibit 1 lists all the states and where they stand in their philosophy of governmental immunity, as of 1971. As stated before, this area of the law is undergoing change, and your state may already have taken a different stand on the problem. You may be doing yourself a service by calling your professional organization to find out if there have been any changes, so that you will be sure you are adequately protected.

Category Two of the chart shows where many of the states take their position. School districts which are in this category will pay for damages caused by their employees, or through their own negligence, only in certain situations. Most of the activities in which schools are involved relate to the school's duty to teach children. If, when carrying out this duty, a duty of the state, an injury occurs through the acts or omission to act by one of the school district's employees, or by the school district itself, the school district cannot be held liable. A school district is *not* liable for "governmental" acts—those acts which are for the purpose of fulfilling the district's obligation to teach children.

On the other hand, if the school district is involved in an activity that is not in the furtherance of its duties as a school district, and is involved in an activity which is for its own convenience or an activity which could be provided by a private third party or corporation, it is involved in a "proprietary" act and can be held liable. The distinction between governmental and proprietary acts is not discussed by most courts, because most acts in which a school is involved could automatically be deemed governmental, depending upon the viewpoint taken. A helpful test is to ask: (1) Is the activity required by state law? If so, it is governmental. (2) Can the activity be done by a third party, or is it for the purpose of saving or raising extra money? If so, it is proprietary.

For example, assume a school district encouraged students to sell breakfast tickets to the community, so that the students could hold dances on Friday nights. In addition, assume the district encouraged use by teachers of their personal automobiles for the purpose of taking students to sell these tickets. Assuming the teacher was negligent, and a student was injured in an accident, it is quite possible that the school district would be ultimately liable for the debt.

This dilemma is further complicated by liability insurance policies. In those states which follow the doctrine of immunity (Category One), the school district cannot buy insurance even if it wants the protection. However, for some of those states which are in Category Two, special statutes have been enacted, permitting the school district to buy liability insurance which covers specific areas such as bus transportation. This does not give the individual teacher a great deal of protection. For those persons teaching in a state in Category Three of the immunity doctrine, unless their district has purchased insurance, the "governmental v. proprietary" problem would be the situation with which they would be faced.

If the state in which a teacher works does not have a statute or a court decision holding the school district liable for its own torts, teachers and administrators alone are personally responsible for damages inflicted on students as a result of their negligent acts or omissions. In Category Three of the immunity doctrine are those states which have such statutes or court decisions transferring the liability from the teacher to the school district in certain circumstances where the district has general liability insurance policies. However, these laws differ in what they cover. Those states that are marked with a "I" generally limit school liability to injuries resulting from transportation accidents. Those states listed with "II" are more general in that they will allow a citizen to sue for specifically named acts that are within the general liability policy of the school district. In addition, these statutes or court decisions will say whether or not liability insurance is required. If the statute leaves the decision to the individual school districts, the district is not obligated to buy insurance. If the district does not, and someone is injured, the district is generally treated as if it were in Category Two of the immunity doctrine. The larger the district, the greater are the possibilities that it has purchased liability insurance. Therefore, the teacher is generally given a great deal of protection from liability for most torts. The insurance purchased does have its limitations. Insurance does not cover all situations, and if the situation is not covered in the policy, the school district is immune from liability. Also, the dollar amount is limited, and generally, the district cannot be held liable for amounts exceeding those limits stipulated in the policy.

As previously stated, you are individually responsible for your own conduct, and you are not protected by the school district unless it is specifically so provided in the laws of the state in which you work. Because of all the students with whom you are involved, and because of all the varied activities in which the students participate, the possibility of your being sued is extremely high. In addition, it is becoming increasingly easier for an injured party to file a lawsuit against a teacher for an alleged wrong. People are probably more involved in the law today than they ever have been in the past. Students are beginning to learn their rights, whereas, in the days of the old school marm, students didn't think they had any. If a child sues a teacher, what can he realistically expect to collect? Teachers are not paid exorbitant salaries, and while the social stigma may be unnerving to the teacher, and the fighting of a lawsuit an irritating experience, the student who has been severely damaged might have to bear much of the loss on his own. Logically, this is not a fair situation, and as a result, general liability insurance has become a favorable protection for teachers to consider. Many states in Category Three automatically give school districts the right to purchase this protection for their employees and themselves. You should avail yourself of this knowledge for your own security.

Laws that protect teachers from liability are often called "save harmless" laws. Stated simply, this means that the public body for which the teacher works (the school district) will save the teacher from harm, and will reimburse and defend him from claims brought against him for acts or omissions committed in the course of his employment. This also means that if a teacher commits an act or omission that is not covered by the law, or if the act that is committed or omitted is a discretionary one on the part of the teacher, liability is strictly upon the shoulders of the one who committed the act. When the act is not within the scope of the school's business, liability will generally be upon the one committing the act, and not his employer.

An example of such a "save harmless" statute is reproduced at the end of this chapter. This statute is much like others which refer to the same problem. The statute is self-explanatory, and covers those areas in which the teacher is protected. These areas involve most situations that a teacher will encounter, and the only serious problem in interpretation is ORS 30.265(d). What is discretionary, and whether or not the discretion is abused, is a constant argument as to liability. Chapter Three will cover most of the problems that you might be faced with when attempting to determine this questions.

States in Category Four of the immunity doctrine have save harmless statutes, and teachers working in those states are protected more than teachers anywhere else. Even though the save harmless statutes have restrictive clauses, and even though the act or omission must be within the teacher's scope of employment, the teacher does have a great deal of protection that others working in different states are not given.

TORT ACTIONS AGAINST PUBLIC BODIES

30.260 Definitions for 30.260 to 30.300. As used in ORS 30.260 to 30.300, unless the context requires otherwise:

(1) "Governing body" means the group or officer in which the controlling authority of any public body is vested.

(2) "Public body" means the state and any department, agency, board or commission of the state, any city, county, school district or other political subdivision or municipal or public corporation and any instrumentality thereof.

[1967 c.627 §1]

30.265 Scope of liability of public body for torts. (1) Subject to the limitations of ORS 30.260 to 30.300, every public body is liable for its torts and those of its officers, employees and agents acting within the scope of their employment or duties, whether arising out of a governmental or proprietary function.

(2) Every public body is immune from liability for:

(a) Any claim for injury to or death of any person or injury to property resulting from an act or omission of an officer, employee or agent of a public body when such officer, employee or agent is immune from liability.

(b) Any claim for injury to or death of any person covered by the Workmen's Compensation Law.

(c) Any claim in connection with the assessment and collection of taxes.

(d) Any claim based upon the performance of or the failure to exercise or perform a discretionary function or duty, whether or not the discretion is abused.

(e) Any claim which is limited or barred by the provisions of any other statute.

(3) Neither a public body nor its officers, employees and agents acting within the scope of their employment or duties are liable for injury or damage:

(a) Arising out of riot, civil commotion or mob action or out of any act or omission in connection with the prevention of any of the foregoing.

(b) Because of an act done or omitted under apparent authority of a law, resolution, rule or regulation which is unconstitutional, invalid or inapplicable except to the extent that they would have been liable had the law, resolution, rule or regulation been constitutional, valid and applicable, unless such act was done or omitted in bad faith or with malice.

(4) ORS 30.260 to 30.300 do not apply to any claim against any public bouy arising before July 1, 1968. Any such claim may be presented and enforced to the same extent and subject to the same procedure and restrictions as if ORS 30.260 to 30.300 had not been adopted.

[1967 c.627 §§2, 3, 10; 1969 c.429 §1]

30.270 Amount of liability. (1) Liability of a public body on claims within the scope of ORS 30.260 to 30.300 shall not exceed:

(a) $25,000 to any claimant for any number of claims for damage to or destruction of property, including consequential damages, arising out of a single accident or occurrence.

(b) $50,000 to any claimant for all other claims arising out of a single accident or occurrence.

(c) $300,000 for any number of claims arising out of a single accident or occurrence.

(2) No award for damages on any such claim shall include punitive damages. The limitation imposed by this section on individual claimants includes damages claimed for loss of services or loss of support arising out of the same tort.

(3) Where the amount awarded to or settled upon multiple claimants exceeds $300,000, any party may apply to any circuit court to apportion to each claimant his proper share of the total amount limited by subsection (1) of this section. The share apportioned each claimant shall be in the proportion that the ratio of the award or settlement made to him bears to the aggregate awards and settlements for all claims arising out of the occurrence. [1967 c.627 §4; 1969 c.429 §2]

30.275 Content of notice of claim; who may present claim; time of notice; time of action. (1) Every person who claims damages from a public body for or on account of any loss or injury within the scope of ORS 30.260 to 30.300 shall cause to be presented to the public body within 180 days after the alleged loss or injury a written notice stating the time, place and circumstances thereof, and the amount of compensation or other relief demanded. Claims against the State of Oregon shall be presented to the state agency against whom the claim is made or to the Attorney General. Claims against any other public body shall be presented to a person upon whom process could be served in accordance with subsection (2) of ORS 15.080. Failure to state the amount of compensation or other relief demanded does not invalidate the notice.

(2) When the claim is for death, the notice may be presented by the personal representative, surviving spouse or next of kin, or by the consular officer of the foreign country of which the deceased was a citizen, within one year after the alleged injury or loss resulting in such death. However, if the person for whose death the claim is made has presented a notice that would have been sufficient had he lived, an action for wrongful death may be brought without any additional notice.

(3) No action shall be maintained unless such notice has been given and unless the action is commenced within two years after the date of such accident or occurrence. The time for giving such notice does not include the time, not exceeding 90 days, during which the person injured is unable to give the notice because of the injury or because of minority, incompetency or other incapacity.
[1967 c.627 §5; 1969 c.429 §3]

30.280 Insurance against liability; effect of insurance; payment of premiums. (1) The governing body of any public body may procure insurance against liability of the public body and its officers, employees and agents.

(2) Such insurance may include coverage for the claims specified in subsection (2) of ORS 30.265. The procurement of such insurance shall not be deemed a waiver of immunity.

(3) If the public body has authority to levy taxes, it may include in its levy an amount to pay the premium costs for such insurance.
[1967 c.627 §6]

30.285 Public body may indemnify public officers. (1) The governing body of any public body may defend, save harmless and indemnify any of its officers, employees and agents, whether elective or appointive, against any tort claim or demand, whether groundless or otherwise, arising out of an alleged act or omission occurring in the performance of duty.

(2) The provisions of subsection (1) of this section do not apply in case of malfeasance in office or wilful or wanton neglect of duty.

(3) This section does not repeal or modify ORS 243.510 to 243.620.
[1967 c.627 §7]

30.290 Settlement of claims; approval of court if settlement more than $2,500. The governing body of any public body may, subject to the provisions of any contract of liability insurance existing, compromise, adjust and settle tort claims against the public body for damages under ORS 30.260 to 30.300 and may, subject to procedural requirements imposed by law or charter, appropriate money for the payment of amounts agreed upon. When the amount of settlement exceeds $2,500, the settlement shall not be effective until approved by the circuit court, unless such settlement is not to be paid from public funds.
[1967 c.627 §8]

30.295 Payment of judgment or settlement; remedies for nonpayment; tax levy for payment. When a judgment is entered against or a settlement is made by a public body for a claim within the scope of ORS 30.260 to 30.300, payment shall be made and the same remedies shall apply in case of nonpayment as in the case of other judgments or settlements against the public body. If the public body has the authority to levy taxes and the judgment or settlement is unpaid at the time of the annual tax levy, the governing body shall, if it finds that other funds are not available for payment of the judgment, levy a tax sufficient to pay the judgment or settlement and interest accruing thereon to the expected time of payment, subject to any levy for debt service and within any limits imposed by law.
[1967 c.627 §9]

30.300 ORS 30.260 to 30.300 exclusive. ORS 30.260 to 30.300 is exclusive and supersedes all home rule charter provisions and conflicting laws and ordinances on the same subject.
[1967 c.627 §11]

FOOTNOTES

1 Gover v. Stovall et. al., 35 S.W. 2d 24, 26 (Ky. 1931).
2 Husser v. School District of Pittsburgh, 228 A.2d 910 (Pa. 1967).
3 228 A.2d 910,911. Dissenting opinion.
4 288 A.2d 910, 911. Dissenting opinion.

TWO

Guarding Against Intentional Injuries to Teachers and Students

When someone violates another's personal rights, he has committed a tort. If this happens, the injured party has a right to be compensated for any harm that has been inflicted. Torts can happen either inadvertently or intentionally. They can also be prevented by following basic guidelines, and by understanding the principles under which they operate.

You will find that:

1. If a person is made afraid for his immediate personal safety, the tort of assualt has occurred.
2. Assault generally precedes a battery, and the latter can sometimes be prevented by taking appropriate steps of discipline at the assault stage.
3. In the school, you are a substitute for the parent. Therefore, you have the power to administer moderate correction to your students.
4. You may detain a student within fixed boundaries.
5. You may temporarily confiscate a student's personal property, but you may not permanently retain possession.
6. Libel and slander should not be condoned anywhere. This includes faculty rooms and administration offices.

In this chapter, all of the torts discussed have the common element of "intent." One must intend the injury, or intend to do an act that is substantially certain to cause damage. Also, if the person who does an act does not believe an injury will result, but an ordinary careful man would realize that such would be the case, intent still exists.

If a person intends to do an act, he is generally responsible for the consequences. This is true even if the intent is not harmful in its nature.

Intentional injuries involve voluntary acts. For example, if a student, as a practical joke, places a mousetrap in your desk and your finger is injured as a result, the student will be liable for intentionally interfering with your right to be free from bodily harm. Although the student may not have intended to injure you, he still intended the act, and should have been able to foresee that an injury could result.

ASSAULTS DO NOT INVOLVE PHYSICAL HARM

An assault is an intentional tort that does not require physical contact. Assault is a tort committed against the *mind* of another. For example, if a student stood in your way and said something, or acted in a manner which reasonably caused you to be in fear of immediate harmful or offensive contact (such as clenching his fist in your face in a threatening way), an assault has been committed. Assault involves fear, *not* contact. Of course, the fear must be reasonable under the circumstances. If the ordinary teacher would be afraid in the same or similar situation, the fear is considered reasonable.

<table>
<tr><td>The Act of
Assault</td><td>The act which evokes fear must be an offer to use force, with the apparent ability and opportunity to immediately follow through with the threat. If such is the case, an assault has been committed.</td></tr>
</table>

When an assault occurs, immediate disciplinary measures should be taken. Many people feel that nothing can be done because there has been no actual injury. This is a major misconception, and can result in serious problems that are easily avoidable. Assault is the forerunner to a battery, and many times it is quite separate in the actual time sequence. If a teacher is blocked in the halls and threatened with possible immediate injury, the student has committed an assault. If the student carries out his threat as by striking the teacher, he has committed a battery, even if the blow is not a hard one or is a glancing one.

In October, 1970, 141 employees were injured in a Chicago school district. Thirteen were injured by parents, 19 were injured by outsiders, and 109 were injured by students.[1] Some of these injuries could have been foreseen. Discipline at the assault stage is the key guideline to follow.

In a Mississippi case, five students used offensive language towards the superintendent, and struck two faculty members.[2] Before the physical contact took place, there were threats or acts which forewarned the injury. The students were suspended after the injury happened. Could the students have been suspended before the actual contact? If the teachers had been assaulted, although not actually physically abused, the students could have been immediately suspended. In other words, if several students surround you, and act as though they are going to harm you—and you reasonably fear that they will, but they do not—you can have them disciplined. In other words, you do not have to be injured before you can discipline students.

The thing to remember is that teachers are going to be assaulted. However, you should be protected when the assault occurs, and not after you have been physically abused. If you are not protected when the action is a mere assault, it not only could cause distrust between you and your administration, but it could also develop into something much more serious and harmful.

PREVENTING HARMFUL OR OFFENSIVE CONTACT

Many times assault and battery are tied together in the same lawsuit, even though they are two distinct and separate torts. The gist of battery is the touch, and is described as:

	1. Unpermitted
The Elements	2. Unprivileged
of Battery	3. Contact with another, in a
	4. Rude or angry manner.

A battery is a violation of another person's right to be free from offensive bodily contact. If there is not an injury when the battery occurs, there is generally no liability, unless there can be shown some sort of mental injury. However, disciplinary action should be taken immediately if a battery does occur, even without injury.

Touching between teachers and students going through the halls is certainly not battery unless the touch is in a rude or angry manner. For example, if a student comes around a corner and accidentally knocks you down, no battery has been committed, but if he intentionally shoves you or trips you, it is a battery.

What might normally be considered a battery if done by someone outside the teaching profession many times is not so considered if done by a teacher. This is true because a teacher has the privilege of discipline due to his legal relationship with his students. The thing to remember is that there are degrees to which a person can go when touching another, and you should know these degrees before you physically discipline a child for a rule that may have been broken. The degrees are expressed in terms of what is reasonably necessary under the circumstances. For example, you should not strike a child for being tardy, but you may do so if the child is setting a fire and physical force is necessary in order to prevent the damage.

The courts are not eager to get into the problems of discipline within the school. If the court does look into a case, it is generally because there has been a flagrant violation of the teacher's privilege, or there is some legal problem unique to the circumstances. Courts leave most of the decisions up to school administrations. Many school districts leave discipline up to the principal; therefore, you do not have to worry about it, except in situations where immediate discipline is necessary. Where this is not the case, you might find yourself in a legal and moral dilemma as to what you can do when disciplining a child.

There are many forms of punishment, and corporal punishment is not desirable except in special cases. In New Jersey and Massachusetts, for example, corporal punishment is prohibited by law. Texas, on the other hand, feels it is justifiable. In many other states, school districts prohibit it in their certified staff policies, or permit corporal punishment only if it is administered by the principal or another teacher.

Corporal punishment has not always been effective in the schools, and might properly be left to the child's parents. Where corporal punishment seems necessary, it should only be administered with the idea of moderately correcting the child. An Alabama court expressed the generally accepted rule that:

**GUIDE
RULE**
... [THE] TEACHER IS, WITHIN REASONABLE BOUNDS, THE SUBSTITUTE FOR THE PARENT ... [AND] IS VESTED WITH THE POWER TO ADMINISTER MODERATE CORRECTION, WITH A PROPER INSTRUMENT, IN CASES OF MISCONDUCT, WHICH OUGHT TO HAVE SOME REFERENCE TO THE CHARACTER OF THE OFFENSE, THE SEX, AGE, SIZE, AND PHYSICAL STRENGTH OF THE PUPIL.[3]

Punishment is used as a means of controlling the student's conduct, and preventing violations of reasonable rules regulating his conduct. One authority justifies it as follows:

Corporal punishment as a means of maintaining control over the pupil is not nearly as prevalent as it once was.... [Most states] leave the matter to the discretion of local school authorities. Almost all states have specific laws forbidding cruelty to children, and school authorities are obligated to make sure that punishment is reasonably proper. If such is not the case, the person administering the punishment is liable on the charge of cruelty to a child or assault and battery.

When is corporal punishment reasonable and proper? The following characteristics of reasonable and proper punishment are offered as guides:

	1. IT IS IN CONFORMANCE WITH STATUTORY ENACTMENTS.
	2. IT IS FOR THE PURPOSE OF CORRECTION AND WITHOUT MALICE.
GUIDE RULE	3. THE PUPIL KNOWS WHEREIN HE HAS ERRED AND IS THUS
FOR	AWARE OF THE REASON FOR THE PUNISHMENT.
CORPORAL	4. IT IS NOT CRUEL NOR EXCESSIVE AND LEAVES NO
PUNISHMENT	PERMANENT MARK OR INJURY.
	5. IT IS SUITED TO THE AGE AND SEX OF THE PUPIL.
	6. IT IS ADMINISTERED IN THE PUPIL-TEACHER RELATIONSHIP.[4]

If you find that corporal punishment is necessary, and you follow these guidelines, you generally cannot be held liable to a student. What your administration thinks about corporal punishment is another matter, and you should consider their attitude toward such action.

In an Illinois case, a teacher was given the duty of keeping crowds away from a fence separating a football field from the stands. When a football player was injured, a group of students went out to the sidelines of the playing field to find out how serious the injuries were. The teacher involved told them to return to their seats. As the students began to return, the teacher allegedly grabbed hold of one of the students, and started hitting him in the face. At the trial, the teacher said he was not guilty of fighting because he was privileged to strike the student, and that, as a teacher, he could use corporal punishment. However, the court found that under the circumstances the teacher was not justified in his actions, and that he had used unreasonable force.[5]

Taking this case and placing it within the guidelines for corporal punishment listed above, you can first see that corporal punishment is allowed in Illinois; therefore, the teacher's act conformed with statutory enactments. In addition, it can be assumed that the teacher's acts were for the purpose of correction. Moreover, the student was probably aware of why he was being punished, in that he was not to go near the football field, and he was to return to the stands when ordered by the teacher. The problem is in item four of the corporal punishment guide listed: the teacher's act of hitting the student in the face was excessive under the circumstances.

In this case, if the teacher had shoved the student toward the stands in a manner that would generally not be harmful, that act may have been considered privileged. Or, had the student hit the teacher in the face, the circumstances would have been changed and a different outcome might be expected.

As a general rule of thumb, a teacher should never hit a student in the face. There are many acts of this nature which have caused permanent injuries, due to "glass jaws" or other ailments that the student might have had prior to the altercation. The fact that the teacher did not know about a student's glass jaw or prior concussion makes no difference. Unless the teacher can show that his act of hitting the student in the face was absolutely necessary and reasonable under the circumstances, he will be held liable.

If a person (student or teacher) exceeds those bounds which are reasonable under the circumstances, liability will be imposed, and the injured party will have a right to compensation in damages for the wrong he has suffered. The test is:

GUIDE RULE

IS THE CONTACT REASONABLE UNDER THE CIRCUM-STANCES? IF THE ANSWER IS THAT THE CONTACT IS REASONABLE, THE TEACHER WILL NOT BE LIABLE. ALTHOUGH OTHER ALTERNATIVES FOR REPRIMANDING THE STUDENT MIGHT BE POSSIBLE, IF THE TEACHER TAKES THE PHYSICAL COURSE IN GOOD FAITH, WITHOUT ILL WILL, AND ACTS REASONABLY, HE WILL NOT BE LIABLE.

This guide rule for corporal punishment is valid, so long as the other considerations heretofore discussed are also present.

The student is not privileged, and he will be liable if he commits a battery. However, teachers seldom sue students. Perhaps the rationale behind this is that most students lack financial means of their own, and teachers often feel that to sue a student is "unprofessional" or "unbecoming." Also, teachers are often compensated for injuries of this nature by workmen's compensation or medical insurance carried by the school district or the teacher himself. Nevertheless, the student would be primarily liable in a civil suit, and in some circumstances might also be criminally liable, or subject to appropriate action in a juvenile court.

WHAT IS MENTAL DISTRESS

The intentional infliction of mental distress does not often involve teachers. However, it is quite possible that this could change. A person has the right to be free from severe emotional distress. If another person violates that right by intentionally inflicting mental distress upon another, the one who has been damaged has the right to be compensated for any physical or mental injuries he has suffered.

In order for a person to get compensation, most courts require that his mental distress be accompanied by a physical injury. This requirement is necessary in order to prevent false lawsuits. Otherwise, it would be difficult to prove the extent of the injury, or even if there was an actual injury that deserved compensation.

Although intentional infliction of mental distress has not often been recognized in the past, it is rapidly gaining greater recognition as more is learned about how the mind functions. The elements of this tort can be summarized as:

Elements of Mental Distress	Conduct which exceeds all bounds tolerated by a decent society, or is of a nature which is especially calculated to cause, and does cause, mental distress of a very serious kind.

The one who, without privilege to do so, intentionally causes such severe emotional distress to another is liable for such emotional stress and any bodily harm resulting from it. This means that your acts or words should not be calculated in a way which will cause the student severe emotional damage. Recognition that liability could be imposed for committing this tort might encourage other forms of discipline.

Tact is a major element to consider, if the persons involved want to avoid liability. This is especially true when an innocent person is accused of doing something wrong, such as stealing, if the school is not absolutely certain as to innocence or guilt. For example, in a Minnesota case, school authorities falsely accused a girl of being "promiscuous." As a result of the statement made to her, the girl suffered severe mental anguish and nervous shock. The student was granted compensation by the court, which said: "If the accusation was false and without justification, there was an invasion of the plaintiff's legal right to be secure in her reputation for virtue . . . ."[6]

Keep this case in mind if you notice that a student's skirt is unduly short, or that a blouse is in poor taste. It is proper for you to discourage what you consider to be immoral behavior or dress. However, if in front of the classroom you refer to the student, and point out how distressing she looks, it would seem possible that your statements are reasonably calculated to cause, and would cause, severe emotional distress to the student. If she did suffer such emotional distress and resulting physical illness, you could be held liable. However, if the student does not suffer any shame, or does not care one way or the other about what was said, there would be no liability on your part. There must be damage, usually physical as well as mental.

TIPS ON DETENTION

Many times, when one of your students breaks a rule, especially at the elementary level, you use detention as a form of punishment. This type of punishment is used to discourage the student from repeating the infraction that caused him to be confined to a certain area for a certain period of time. You are privileged to use this form of punishment when it is reasonable and for a good and definite purpose.

When you tell a first grader he cannot go out to recess with the other children until he has finished his assignment, or because the child pulled another student's hair, detention is an acceptable disciplinary action However, detention of a student must be carried out under proper conditions and with proper care and discretion. For example, it would be unreasonable for you to detain a child during the lunch period for one month without letting him get something to eat. On the other hand, it would generally be reasonable for you to prevent a child from going to "brunch," and recess, or for you to require the child to stay after school for a reasonable length of time, if he has a way of getting home after the buses have left.

When the child comes to school, he comes under the jurisdiction of the rules governing the school's activities and students. Students may, therefore, be forced to stay within the confines of the school grounds for the entire time that school is in session. This is true, even though the student might want to go to eat lunch at the hamburger stand down the street. Such rules are valid because they are intended to protect the students' safety.

The rules discussed are reasonable because they are necessary as disciplinary measures, or for the students' safety, but there are times when restrictions placed upon the student's freedom of movement constitutes false imprisonment. This tort consists of:

	1. Confinement
Elements of	2. Within boundaries
False	3. Stipulated by the teacher
Imprisonment	4. Without authority.

Problems in this tort are generally related to attempting to determine if the teacher had the authority to fix certain boundaries, or if that authority was exceeded. Confinement of a student is appropriate if it is reasonable under the circumstances. If confinement is the result of ill will or vindictiveness on the part of the teacher, or is used to enforce an unlawful rule, it is clearly unreasonable. If the ordinary teacher would have done the same thing, or if the ordinary teacher would believe that the acts which resulted in the confinement justified such steps, the teacher who confined the student within set boundaries will not be liable.

There is a difference between the rights of a public school teacher or student, and the private school teacher or student. In the private school, the administration has much more authority. If the parent of the student does not like the rules that are imposed by the private institution, he generally has few remedies other than withdrawing the child and placing him in another school. A private school has more rights and powers, for reasons too numerous to delve into here. However, the main reason is probably the fact that a student is not obligated to go to a private school, so his legal relationship with the school is on a different basis.

In one related instance a false imprisonment and cruelty question was raised at a private school, where the administration found that, by placing the child in a large box, without light and without access to the outside, the child was calmed down and motivated to behave. The box was generally used for those who were too hyperactive to fit in successfully with the rest of their environment. Although this type of treatment nearly hit the level beyond which even a private institution can go, it was still considered a valid method of treatment for the child. This was true for the private school, but if a teacher in a public school decided to build such a box for her first graders, she would be liable for falsely imprisoning any students she forced into the box. She would also be liable for intentionally inflicting mental distress, if that were the result.

STUDENTS' PROPERTY IS PERSONAL

Students often bring personal possessions to school. Some of these items interfere with the smooth operation of your classroom; therefore, you will have the student put the property away, or else you hold the property for him. Generally, the property is returned to the student and there are no problems. Nevertheless, when the school year is done, many teachers can be found emptying their desks and closets of assorted "contraband."

Improper retention of these items is a tort called trespass to personal property. The tort is:

	1. The intentional
Elements of	2. Interference with the
Trespass to	3. Possession or
Personal	4. Physical condition of the
Property	5. Personal property of another
	6. Without justification.

In order for you to be liable for this tort, you must generally cause some damage to the property in question. However, if you do not damage the property, but you wrongfully retain it for an unreasonable time, you must pay the student what the property is worth.

Because of your relationship with the student, you are justified in taking things away from students that either interfere with your attempt to maintain your classroom in an orderly manner, or could be a threat to the well-being of other students. This is generally left to the discretion of the teacher, and the tort does not come into question in too many instances. The gist of the problem is that:

GUIDE **RULE**	YOU MAY HAVE THE RIGHT TO TAKE PROPERTY AWAY FROM YOUR STUDENTS, BUT YOU DO NOT HAVE THE RIGHT TO KEEP THE PROPERTY FOR YOUR OWN USE, OR TO KEEP THE PROPERTY AWAY FROM YOUR STUDENTS FOR AN UNREASONABLE LENGTH OF TIME.

Of course, it depends on the type of property. If the property is illegal contraband, you have an obligation to take the property to the principal, and he should handle the situation from there. But if the property in question is, for instance, a squirt-gun, it belongs to the student, and should be returned to him with instructions not to bring it back to school. If the student does bring it back to school, you still have no right to the property but must follow other disciplinary procedures.

Cases have come into the courts where protest materials have been confiscated. There have been instances where the school administration has seized controversial underground newspapers. Since such material is allowable on campus, the school administration has no right to retain possession (Chapter Nine). In cases of "protest buttons," you may or may not be able to force their removal. This will depend upon the circumstances. However, one thing is certain—you are not justified in tearing the button from the student's shirt and refusing to return it. The property belongs to the one who owns it, and the one who owns the property has the right to ultimate possession. If you interfere with that right for an unreasonable time, or for an unreasonable reason, you are liable for the value of the property to the owner.

SLANDER WITHIN THE SCHOOL BUILDING

A tremendous number of slanderous statements are made in the faculty rooms of the schools. Defamation is a complicated area, involving words, gestures, privileges and opinions. What may be a defamatory remark to one person may, at times, not be to another. Possibly, it could be said that defamatory remarks are those statements which falsely impute that the one being defamed has done something, or has had something done to him, that would exceed all bounds tolerated by a decent society. At times, there must be an injury, and at other times, it does not matter if the one defamed was injured or not. There are times when one has a qualified privilege to defame another, and there are times when one is completely immune. Some people can say things about others that a third person could not say without being slanderous. A "third person" is how teachers would generally be considered in most circumstances. Slander consists of derogatory "spoken" words. Libel consists of published or written words.

As you can see, it is difficult to attempt to define precisely "defamation," but as a noted legal writer states:

> A defamatory communication usually has been defined as one which tends to hold the plaintiff up to hatred, contempt or ridicule, or to cause him to be shunned or avoided. This definition is certainly too narrow, since an imputation of insanity, or poverty, or an assertion that a woman has been raped, which would be likely to arouse only pity or sympathy in the minds of all decent people, have been held to be defamatory. [Rather]:

GUIDE RULE   DEFAMATION IS . . . THAT WHICH TENDS TO INJURE "REPUTATION" IN THE POPULAR SENSE; TO DIMINISH THE ESTEEM, RESPECT, GOOD WILL OR CONFIDENCE IN WHICH THE PLANTIFF IS HELD, OR TO EXCITE ADVERSE, DEROGATORY OR UNPLEASANT FEELINGS OR OPINIONS AGAINST HIM . . . .

> . . . [It] is defamatory upon its face to say that the plaintiff has attempted suicide, that he refuses to pay his just debts, that he is immoral or unchaste, or "queer," or has made improper advances to women, or is having "wife trouble" and is about to be divorced; that he is . . . an anarchist . . . a bastard [or] a eunuch . . . because all of these things obviously tend to affect the esteem in which he is held by his neighbors.[7]

Slander suits would be much more common if the people defamed knew about the things being said.

GUIDE RULE   ONE IS DEFAMED AND INJURED IF HE IS LOWERED IN THE ESTEEM OF ANY SUBSTANTIAL AND RESPECTABLE GROUP, EVEN THOUGH IT MAY BE QUITE A SMALL MINORITY.

If defamatory remarks are made to six teachers about a student, the six would probably be considered a substantial group. Even three teachers might be considered a substantial group, depending on the size of the school in which they worked, and depending upon the other teachers' relationship with the student or teacher being defamed. In some instances, even one person might be enough.

Not all statements are sufficient to hold a person liable for slander, and a teacher has a qualified privilege to make a statement if it is for the purpose of conveying important information to the administration or to the child's parent. In other words:

GUIDE RULE   IF THE DEFAMATORY STATEMENT IS MADE WITHIN PROPER ADMINISTRATIVE CHANNELS, THE TEACHER CANNOT BE HELD LIABLE IF HE IS ACTING IN GOOD FAITH. BUT IF THE STATEMENT IS GOSSIP, OR IF IT IS MADE IN THE PRESENCE OF OTHER STUDENTS, EVEN THOUGH SPOKEN TO AND ABOUT THE STUDENT BEING DEFAMED, THE PERSON MAKING THE STATEMENT MAY BE HELD LIABLE.

Administrators have more leeway than do teachers. In one case, the president of Transylvania University was sued for alleged libelous remarks made by the president to a student's father. The facts of this case show that the president of the college had received complaints to the effect that the student had been acting in an immoral manner by indecently exposing himself from the college dormitory window. The complaints were investigated, and proved to be correct. Thereupon, the president expelled the student, and wrote the boy's father, explaining his reasons for the dismissal. Upon receipt of the letter, and after a great deal of argument, the father sued the president. In finding for the president, the court said that he was privileged to say what he did. The statements in the case were made in good faith, without malice, and in answer to a valid inquiry. Furthermore, the president was acting within the scope of his duty towards the community. He believed the communication was true, and there were valid grounds on which to base his belief.[8]

GUIDE RULE   IF A SLANDEROUS STATEMENT IS TO BE MADE WITHOUT LIABILITY, IT MUST BE MADE IN GOOD FAITH, BASED UPON REASONABLE GROUNDS, AND MADE DURING A PROPER OCCASION, WITH A PROPER MOTIVE, AND IN A PROPER MANNER.

HOW THE TEACHER CAN PROTECT HIMSELF FROM LIABILITY

There are many situations which require you to take affirmative action. Sometimes you act in the way you feel is necessary, but in a way which others might consider improper or invalid. When this happens, you must occasionally justify your acts to your principal or to a parent.

Probably the oldest defense in education is *in loco parentis*. This concept means that:

GUIDE **RULE**	WHILE ACTING WITHIN THE SCOPE OF YOUR DUTY, YOU STAND IN THE SHOES OF THE PARENT; THEREFORE, YOU MAY GENERALLY EXERCISE SUCH POWERS AS THE PARENT WOULD EXERCISE OVER THE STUDENT.

In loco parentis gives you the right to reasonably demand from the student certain forms of conduct which you feel are necessary. In addition, you have the right to discipline the student, and to specify the type of work performance required.

GUIDE **RULE**	THE PARENT OF THE CHILD IS POWERLESS TO INTERFERE IN SCHOOL MATTERS THAT ARE REASONABLE AND FOR THE PURPOSE OF EDUCATION. THEREFORE, IF YOU COMMIT AN ACT WHICH AFFRONTS A PARENT, THE ACT IS VALID IF IT IS REASONABLE AND WITHIN THE SCOPE OF YOUR DUTY.

There are limitations to the concept of *in loco parentis*. Although you stand in place of the parent, you are not the parent in situations not related to school matters. This fact is illustrated by an actual case in which a student came to school with an infected finger. The teacher wanted to help cure the infection, and placed the child's hand in scalding water for ten minutes. The student did not consent to this act, and in fact, another teacher was needed to help hold the hand. Although the infection may have been cured, the child spent 28 days in the hospital, and the act resulted in a permanently scarred and disfigured hand. The teachers attempted to justify their action on the theory of *in loco parentis*. However, the court said:

> These teachers stood *in loco parentis* to the child, but there is nothing in that relationship which will justify [the teachers'] acts. Under the delegated parental authority implied from the relationship of teacher and pupil, a teacher may inflict reasonable corporal punishment on a pupil to enforce discipline. . .but there is no implied delegation of authority to exercise her lay judgment, as a parent may, in a matter of the treatment of injury or disease suffered by a pupil. Treatment of the minor plaintiff's hand was not necessary in this case; [the teachers] were not acting in an emergency . . . The status of a parent, with some of the parent's privileges, is given a school teacher by law in aid of the education and training of the child . . . and ordinarily does not extend beyond matters of conduct and discipline.[9]

GUIDE
RULE

YOU HAVE THE POWERS OF A PARENT IN SCHOOL RELATED MATTERS OF: WORK PERFORMANCE; STUDENT CONDUCT; DISCIPLINE; AND YOUR STUDENTS' IMMEDIATE WELFARE.

In addition to being *in loco parentis,* you have other defenses which might justify an act that has come into question. You have the right to use force when you are defending school property, other people or yourself.

If you walk into a rest room and see students tearing down a towel rack, you cannot strike the students without first asking them to stop what they are doing. If the students do not stop, you may use reasonable force to prevent further destruction of school property.

You can sometimes justify your actions on the grounds that you were protecting another person. If you see two students fighting, you can use necessary force to break up the fight. The force must be reasonable under the circumstances, and not intended to inflict permanent injury.

Using force against a student is also a valid defense when you are protecting yourself. If a student attacks you, you may generally use whatever force is necessary to repel the attack. Again, the force used must be reasonable, and if you act as another teacher would act under the same or similar circumstances, your actions will probably be considered justified.

SUMMARY

The teacher-student relationship should now be easier to understand. Understanding the relationship should eliminate any notion that you are helpless to defend yourself or to discipline a child where such an action is necessary. The circumstances surrounding your acts are important, and they must be considered as various situations arise.

Immediate disciplinary action should be taken the moment an assault occurs, and before someone is seriously injured. An assault does not involve contact, and there is no need to be afraid to walk into your classroom, or in the hallways. Furthermore, there is no need for you to fear reprimanding a student who has broken a valid rule or regulation set by the administration or yourself.

As a general rule, when one person strikes another in a rude or angry manner, a battery has been committed. However, because you are a teacher, your position gives you certain privileges. You are, within reasonable bounds, a substitute for the parent, and you may use moderate physical correction in many instances. You should be able to justify your actions as being reasonably proper under the circumstances. If your physical contact was necessary for correction, was not excessive, and was administered within the teacher-pupil relationship, your actions will generally be considered valid. There are guidelines for you to follow, and you should try not to exceed your authority.

When talking to or about students, you should consider the emotional damage that your words might cause. You must be tactful in what you say, if you want to avoid mental injuries. If a student is emotionally damaged, and there is also a resulting physical injury because of what you said, you will be liable, unless you can show that your statements were not reasonably calculated to cause the emotional distress.

There will be times when you will be asked to talk about a student or colleague. You must avoid slanderous statements. Tact is again important, and you must act in good faith, and within proper administrative channels. Your statements must be based upon reasonable grounds, made with a proper motive, and in a proper manner. You should never knowingly make false statements about anyone.

You may use detention as a form of discipline. The detention must be carried out under proper conditions, and must be reasonable under the circumstances.

Students have the right to keep the property that belongs to them. You may temporarily detain property that interferes with your class or activities, but it must be returned within a reasonable time. This does not mean you may not confiscate illegal materials from your students. This may be done, and you should turn such illegal property over to the school administration.

No doubt torts will occur within your school. Hopefully, you will be able to foresee many of these acts, and thus prevent them from becoming more serious. By understanding your duties and rights within the school building, you will be guarding against intentional injuries to teachers and students.

FOOTNOTES

1 Assault report sent to Chicago Board of Education by Dr. James F. Redmond, General Superintendent of Schools (1970).
2 Brown v. Greer, 296 F. Supp. 595 (U.S. Dist. Ct., Miss. 1969).
3 Boyd v. State, 7 So. 268, 269 (Ala. 1890).
4 Sumption, M.R. "The Control of Pupil Conduct by the School," 20 Law and Contemp. Prob. 80, 88 (1955).
5 City of Macomb v. Gould, 244 N.E.2d 634 (Ill. 1969).
6 Johnson v. Sampson, 208 N.W. 814, 816 (Minn. 1926).
7 Prosser, William L., Law of Torts (3rd Ed. 1964), West Publishing Co., St. Paul, Minn., pp. 756-758.
8 Baskett v. Crossfield, 228 S.W. 673 (Ky. 1921).
9 Guerrieri v. Tyson, 24 A. 2d 468, 469 (Pa. 1942).

THREE

Preventing Negligent Injuries Resulting from School Activities

WHAT CONSTITUTES NEGLIGENCE?

The majority of lawsuits brought against teachers allege that the teacher was somehow negligent in his conduct towards the injured student. Negligence is an illusive term that escapes precise definition. Yet, you know that you must be careful while carrying out your duties, and if you are not careful, there is a possibility that you may be sued. What is careful? How important is the age of your students, and what activities should you supervise more closely? Are some teachers more susceptible to lawsuits than others? What are the more important circumstances for you to consider?

The answers to these questions and many others change so often that the average teacher is in a state of chaos when trying to decide, for instance, whether she should take her students on a field trip or allow them to jump on a trampoline. Negligence depends upon the individual facts and circumstances of the case, and the outcome will vary according to how these facts and circumstances are combined.

Generally:

1. You may be liable where you have failed to ensure the safety of your students.
2. You must explain your rules to your students, and you must enforce them at all times.
3. You must act in the way a reasonable and prudent teacher would act in the same situation.
4. You must eliminate dangerous conditions or activities in cases where a future accident can easily be foreseen.
5. Although a student may have been careless and contributed to an injury, you may still be liable.

**GUIDE
RULE**

NEGLIGENCE EXISTS WHERE THE ACTIVITY OR CONDUCT ON THE PART OF THE TEACHER CREATES AN UNREASONABLE CHANCE OF DANGER. WHEN THE TEACHER IGNORES THE DANGER, OR DOES NOT SEE THE DANGER WHEN HE SHOULD, HE MAY BE HELD NEGLIGENT IF SOMEONE IS INJURED AS A RESULT.

Every year there are cases involving teachers' negligence, and in most instances, you can almost guess the outcome with reasonable certainty. If a teacher throws a pencil at a student whose head is temporarily turned, and the pencil hits the student's eye when he looks back, it is likely that the teacher will be held liable. If a teacher permits students to box without instruction, one student being two feet taller and one hundred pounds heavier than the other, it is likely that the teacher could be held liable for any resulting injury.

Negligence is: *not doing something which the reasonable teacher, considering the circumstances, would ordinarily do;* or *doing something which the ordinary teacher of reason and prudence would not do.*

As mentioned in the discussion of torts in Chapter One, there are four necessary elements in the tort called negligence. They are: (1) Duty; (2) Violation; (3) Cause, and (4) Injury. If any of these elements are missing, you cannot be held liable.

Negligence results when you fail to care for your students as the reasonable teacher would, and as a result of this lack of care, a student is injured. You have the responsibility of ensuring your students' safety in the environment in which the student is attempting to learn and in the activities in which the student is involved. If you negligently fail to fulfill this duty, and someone is injured as a result, it follows that you should be responsible for the damages that occur. There are many terms which could be used to help to describe what negligence consists of; some of these are *carelessness, inattentiveness,* and *lack of diligence or discretion.*

What constitutes a violation of duty depends upon the particular facts and circumstances of the case. Assume, for the purpose of example, that we have three teachers, each desiring to plan a field trip for the class: Miss Lavier, with a third grade class; Mr. Davis, teaching high school sophomores; and Mr. Scotty, who also teaches sophomores. However, Mr. Scotty's students are basically juvenile delinquents with a history of destruction. The three teachers, in taking their classes on a field trip to study nature, must decide whether to go to the beach, to a large field near the school, or to the mountains. Each of the three teachers, in preparation for a field trip, has a separate set of factors to take into consideration. First, consider Miss Lavier.

In Miss Lavier's case, there is more responsibility placed upon her shoulders because of the age of her students. Being eight or nine years old, the students cannot have the intelligence and responsibility of those who are older. Therefore, Miss Lavier must take better care of her students, must supervise them more closely, and must use more discretion in deciding where to go on the field trip. Her "duty" entails more attention; therefore, the field near the school would be the safest place for the children to go. The beach would demand more attention, but might also be reasonably safe if the number of students is not too great, or if she can get help from others and thereby lower the student-supervisor ratio. However, mountain climbing would seem unreasonable, considering the age of the students, and such a trip should be left to a teacher at an upper grade level.

Assuming Miss Lavier does take the children to the beach, she must make sure that she does not violate her duty of caring for the children on the trip. In an actual case of this sort, the teacher permitted a student to stand on a log while the teacher took a picture. Before the picture could be snapped, the ocean waves came into shore and the student was seriously injured when he was swept under the water. This act on the part of the teacher was a violation of the care required. Therefore, the teacher was liable for the injuries that were caused.[1]

Mr. Davis, Teacher No. 2, is in a better situation than that of Miss Lavier. Because his students are older they are more responsible for their own care. However, he still has the duty of supervising the students' activities, and if they go to the mountains, and he observes a few boys standing too close to the edge or swinging across deep crevices, it would be his duty to stop the students from endangering themselves. What might be reasonable for Mr. Davis is not necessarily reasonable for Miss Lavier, because the circumstances have changed, and other factors are to be considered.

Mr. Scotty is in still another situation. It is true that the duty he has toward his students is nearly the same as that of Mr. Davis, but Mr. Scotty, in addition, owes a duty to the community. In general, it can be said that everyone owes all other persons a duty not to subject them to an unreasonable risk of harm. If this class goes to the beach where other people are present, with the students' history of delinquency, Mr. Scotty could be breaching his duty if adequate supervision is not provided. It would seem, therefore, that Mr. Scotty must plan a carefully supervised trip, in order for him to protect the safety of his students and the general public.

The question in negligence is: "What acts or omissions are reasonable under the same or similar circumstances?" If you answer this question in good faith, and in the same way that an ordinary teacher of prudence would do so, you are generally safe from liability and can continue to act or omit to act in the way that you deem necessary.

ENFORCING RULES OF SAFETY IN SCHOOL ACTIVITIES

In every school there are rules which regulate student conduct. These rules are made. for the purpose of helping to carry out the school's educational goals, as well as for the purpose of ensuring the student's safety while he is under the control of the school administration and the classroom teacher.

For rules to validly control student conduct, they must be lawful and reasonable. A rule requiring children to wear adhesive tape over their mouths from the moment they walk into the classroom until the last bell rings, might be considered by a few as being conducive to learning, but it is not reasonable. A rule, even though it might be considered reasonable and lawful, cannot be arbitrarily made. During the "moratorium" demonstrations in 1970, for example, there were many students who felt it was necessary for them to participate in marches during school hours. Valid rules against skipping school exist, and they generally prescribe disciplinary measures to be taken against those who violate those rules. However, there were some teachers so opposed to what the demonstrations represented that they felt it necessary to make some "new" rules. In one illustration, a teacher told his students that if any student missed the teacher's class on that day, the student would automatically fail the course for the entire semester. To help instigate this rule, the teacher moved a previously scheduled test up one week, and demanded doctors' statements from any who might happen to be sick. This new rule was for the day of the moratorium only. It was therefore arbitrary, and could not have been upheld had someone wanted to contest it. (It also was in violation of the students' constitutional rights, as Chapter Nine will explain.) As a Wisconsin court said:

> **GUIDE**
> **RULE**
> ... [A]NY RULE OR REGULATION WHICH HAS FOR ITS OBJECT ANYTHING OUTSIDE OF THE INSTRUCTION OF THE PUPIL—THE [NECESSARY] REQUISITE FOR INSTRUCTION— IS BEYOND THE PROVINCE OF THE BOARD OF EDUCATION TO ADOPT.[2]

Valid rules are those which are necessary to protect the health, morals and safety of the students, or are disciplinary rules which facilitate maintenance of an atmosphere conducive to learning.

There are three main bodies that make rules which govern the student's conduct. The state has set up certain guidelines that every school district must follow. In addition, school boards and administrations set up other rules that they feel are necessary in order to carry out their objectives. These rules are generally directives which fit certain circumstances peculiar to the district involved. For example, a school district in Michigan might require elementary students to wear warm caps during recess in the winter, whereas in California that rule would seem unreasonable.

Teachers make up the third body of rule makers over students. Every teacher has different ways of controlling his or her class, and therefore makes up different regulations governing students' conduct while under his or her authority. You have the right to demand certain forms of behavior from your students, but you cannot make up rules that conflict with rules made by the district or the state. Generally, you cannot govern students' dress, outside activities, or what the students might be doing when they are not under your supervision. You may give homework and require that it be handed in on the following day, but you cannot demand that the homework be completed between the hours of 6:00 P.M. and 7:00 P.M. In other words, you may also make rules, but those rules must be within the scope of your duty and not within the more general scope of the school district or the state.

Rules govern conduct, and the student should be informed what the rules are. Although ignorance is not a defense for adults driving over the speed limit, ignorance does seem to be a defense in holding a teacher liable for injuries that were partly caused by the student's not knowing what the rules were. In a case where a student was injured by an iceball, for example, the district was made liable when a child was injured. In this case, it was held that the students lacked proper supervision, and that the school authorities should have recognized the danger of the snow.[3] On the other hand, in a different case, a student suffered a serious eye injury from a snowball thrown by another student. This case, however, did not impose liability because there was a rule governing snowball throwing, and the students had been warned not to violate this school policy. The court said:

> If a school is to become liable to one pupil for a snowball thrown at him by a fellow pupil, the rule governing such responsibility should be laid down clearly, and be precise enough to be generally understood in the schools.[4]
>
> . . .
>
> Teachers have watched over the play of their pupils time out of mind. At recess periods, not less than in the class room, a teacher owes it to his charges to exercise such care of them as a parent of ordinary prudence would observe in comparable circumstances.[5]

This case points out that you should stop dangerous activities when you recognize their hazardous potential. You must consider the conditions and intervene where there is a foreseeable risk of injury. If you have safety rules governing student conduct, and the students know about these rules, you are safeguarding against personal liability.

The importance of making and enforcing rules of safety can be further seen in a case where an eight-year-old student was playing as he waited for the buses to arrive and take him home. This student was under the supervision of older students who wandered off and left the child unsupervised for a short time. While the older students were gone, the youngster got into a fight, and when he was on the ground, he was injured by a bicycle being ridden by an older student. In finding the school district liable, the court held that not only did lack of supervision play a determining role as to liability, but the school district's failure to have any rules governing the safety of students around bicycle riders amounted to negligence.[6] This seems to imply that had there been rules regulating where students could ride their bikes, and had these rules been impressed upon the students, no liability would have existed on the part of the school district.

This need for rules can also be illustrated by a New Jersey case in which the principal in charge of supervision was held liable to an injured student. In this case, a nine-year-old student was injured as he rounded the corner of a school building and was struck by a paper clip. An older boy had shot the paper clip from a rubber band as he waited to board a school bus taking him to another school. The older boy had a history of being rowdy and a bully, and had hit another student with a paper clip just five minutes before.

It was customary for students to gather around these premises before school actually started. The principal took charge of their supervision, but had not announced any rules regulating their conduct during this period. No teachers were assigned supervisory duty, and he took the full responsibility.

The court said that the principal was negligent in not taking any safety measures toward overseeing the students' presence and their activities. At the time of the accident, the principal had been supervising a milk delivery.

The court also said that:

GUIDE RULE
THE DUTY OF SCHOOL PERSONNEL TO EXERCISE REASONABLE SUPERVISORY CARE FOR THE SAFETY OF STUDENTS ENTRUSTED TO THEM, AND THEIR ACCOUNTABILITY FOR INJURIES RESULTING FROM FAILURE TO DISCHARGE THAT DUTY, ARE WELL RECOGNIZED IN OUR STATE AND ELSEWHERE.[7]

These cases have important implications to teachers involved in supervisory duties and to teachers working in a classroom that has inherent dangers. A vocational education teacher must not only have safety rules, but he must make reasonable efforts to make certain that his students are aware of the regulations, the importance of the regulations, and why they are required.

GUIDE
RULE

IF A RULE IS BROKEN, STEPS MUST BE TAKEN TO ASSURE THAT THE INFRACTION WILL NOT OCCUR A SECOND TIME. IF A TEACHER DOES NOT TAKE FURTHER STEPS, HE MIGHT BE FOUND LIABLE ON THE GROUNDS THAT THE RULE DID NOT REALLY EXIST, EXCEPT ON PAPER.

All vocational instructors must be especially aware of this added responsibility.

Teachers of physical education courses should also recognize the importance of teaching students the rules of safety that regulate the students' activities while they are in class. Not running in the shower room, not tackling during a touch football game, and not swinging baseball bats in the dug-out are rules that must be *enforced*. There are many others, and a one-day lesson plan covering this subject might prove to be an invaluable safety precaution for the teacher as well as the students.

Teachers in other subjects are also obligated to tell students about the rules governing their conduct. Safety rules before field trips, rules regarding chemicals and experiments in science courses and homemaking, and playground conduct rules during recess should be explained to the students by the supervising teacher. The effort may not always save you from liability, but it seems quite possible that the extra effort could either prevent injuries that might occur, or lessen your chances of being sued for negligence.

NEGLIGENCE AND YOUR LIABILITY

What are some of the situations in which you can be held liable for negligence?

1. A vocational or science instructor may be liable where a student is injured and has not been instructed in the use, safety devices, and rules and regulations governing the use of the vocational machinery or scientific chemicals.[8]
2. A physical education teacher may be liable for not properly supervising gymnastic activities, and for not providing safety pads and matting where such equipment is foreseeably necessary.[9]
3. A teacher may be liable for improper medical treatment where he is not acting in an emergency, and the treatment is not immediately necessary.[10]
4. A teacher may be expected to give *personal* instruction to students who have a difficult time in performing particular exercises.[11]
5. Making students do exercises that are not suitable to their age, sex, physical or

mental capabilities can bring about liability. This is especially true in gymnastic activities such as rope climbing exercises and tumbling.[12]

6. Disciplinary actions such as lifting, shaking and dropping etc., a student might be considered excessive if an injury results.[13]

7. A teacher might be held liable where a student is sent on the teacher's personal errand, with directions on how to do the task, and an injury results from the activity. Moreover, liability is especially imposed where an accident is foreseeable.[14]

8. You can be liable where you do not give or get prompt medical attention where the ordinary prudent layman would know that such attention is necessary. You could be liable for any injury that resulted from your unreasonable mistreatment or delay.

9. A football or basketball coach, etc., can sometimes be liable in failing to supervise the removal of an injured player, where the lack of supervision causes or augments an injury.

Most teachers have been held liable for negligence in cases where they have not fulfilled their supervisory duties. Supervision is important, and must be taken seriously; you are the students' guardian, and must fulfill this duty with the utmost prudence.

WHO IS THE "REASONABLE" TEACHER

One of the most important concepts in tort law is the so called "reasonable and prudent man under the same or similar circumstances." "Reasonable" is a difficult word when trying to apply it to teachers. Because teachers follow varied teaching concepts, there seem to be different standards of reasonableness applied to different circumstances. This is not necessarily a bad situation, but it is one which needs to be taken into account. You are considered "reasonable" if what you do or fail to do is something that other teachers like yourself would do or fail to do in like circumstances. However, merely knowing one teacher who would act the same way in the same situation does not free you from liability. You must either act the way the majority of teachers would act, or else you must act in the way a *substantial* minority would act. If such is not the case, generally your act or omission will be a violation of the duty you owe to others.

Circumstances play an important role. Even though the majority of teachers might work in large cities, the teacher working in a one room schoolhouse is held to a different standard of conduct, which is determined by the conduct of teachers in the same type of environment. It might be reasonable for a mid-west teacher in a country area to permit students to play with horses during their lunch break, but it would not be reasonable to allow kids in Chicago to do the same thing if they have not been around horses before.

The essence of negligence is the lack of properly taking care of the children in the way that would ordinarily be expected. The reasonable man does not exist except as a fictitious person to whom ordinary acceptable standards are applied. This does not mean what the "perfect" teacher would have done. Everyone makes mistakes in judgment, and no one should be held liable for such a mistake unless the mistake is unreasonable. In other words:

GUIDE
RULE
WHAT THE ORDINARY TEACHER WOULD DO IS CON-SIDERED REASONABLE; AND EVEN IF THERE WERE SEV-ERAL DIFFERENT ACTS LEFT OPEN FOR A DECISION, IF ALL OF THE ACTS ARE REASONABLE, BUT ONE ACT AS HINDSIGHT WOULD HAVE PROVEN TO BE THE BETTER COURSE OF ACTION, THEN THE ACT THAT THE TEACHER CHOSE IS STILL VALID.

In order to be more precise as to what actually constitutes the reasonable teacher, you should know what some of the physical characteristics are. The teacher who is confined to a wheelchair is not held to the same standard as the teacher who walks. Therefore, the disabled are held to the standard of another who is disabled. This fact might also mean that one confined to a wheelchair should not be given duties which might require him to walk. The imposition of such duties would probably amount to negligence on the part of the administration.

Although the court will look at the teacher's physical condition, it does not generally attempt to determine differences in mental capacity. Justice Holmes wrote:

> The law takes no account of the infinite varieties of temperament, intellect, and education which make the internal character of a given act so different in different men. It does not attempt to see men as God sees them, for more than one sufficient reason.[15]

In other words, you are not free from liability just because you might not be as intelligent as another. If you make a mistake in judgment, it cannot be blamed upon your lack of intelligence; in fact, the law requires that you possess a greater degree of knowledge and skill in relation to caring for children than the ordinary man in the street. The care required is not that of the ordinary man, but that of the ordinary teacher.

For example, in one case, the custodian was placed in charge of supervising children during their free time after they had eaten lunch and the bell for the next period had not yet rung.   When a child was injured, the court held that the school was negligent because the children were not given the care required and expected.[16] This means that giving supervision responsibilities to older students may be considered negligence if the supervision required is that of one who is supposed to be trained. You should consider this when turning the class over to an aide, or to one of your students.

There are still other factors to consider when discussing the standard of the reasonable teacher. In most instances, the standard of care required by the teacher will remain constant. However, if an emergency develops, the courts will sometimes lower the standard normally required, and look to see if the teacher's actions were reasonable under the circumstances. It is much like trying to find a way to "forgive" the teacher for not maintaining the standard that should have been present under normal circumstances.

This is a difficult area that remains indefinite. There are some situations in which you are expected to anticipate an emergency occurring. If you notice children throwing rocks at one another, it would normally be anticipated that one of the children might get injured. With all of the different variables for you to consider, there still remains the main question to ask:

> What would the ordinary teacher who possesses the normal amount of reason and prudence do under the same or similar circumstances?

The answer to that question should give direction as to what course of action the courts and administrations would recognize as being most reasonable.

FORESEEING ACCIDENTS

Not all injuries that happen in the schools are the result of negligence on the part of the teacher. Many times you have nothing to do with a situation. At other times, even though you are present, an accident occurs, due to a condition over which you have no control. The mere fact that you are in control of students does not make you liable unless it can be shown that you were acting in an unreasonable manner. Your authority must be asserted, but you cannot be everywhere at the same time.

An accident is an event resulting from:

1. Carelessness,
2. Ignorance, or
3. Unavoidable causes, which are
4. Unforeseen.

You have a great many obligations in relation to three of the elements in an accident. If you do not fulfill these obligations, there is a chance for liability.

Carelessness:

If you are careless to the extent of being negligent, you are liable if someone is injured as a result. There are many ways in which you can be considered careless. There can be carelessness in your own conduct, as well as in your duty to control or supervise the conduct of children. Again, conduct to be acceptable must be reasonable. For example, you may leave your students alone in the classroom for short periods of time. Leaving the class alone for two minutes while you get supplies might be considered careless, but it would generally not be considered negligent or unreasonable. However, leaving the class alone for twenty minutes in order to socialize is not only careless, but might be considered negligent.

The careless teacher is not liable unless it can be shown that he was also negligent. A case might help to clear up this distinction. In New York, a teacher was absent from her room while placing supplies in a closet. During the short interval, one child threw a pencil to another, but injured the eye of a third student instead. The injured student attempted to hold the teacher liable, but failed. The court held that the teacher's absence was not the cause of the injury. Even if the teacher had been in the room, the accident could still have occurred, and it was not unreasonable for the teacher to act as she did.[17]

There are court decisions which state that:

GUIDE RULE

> BEFORE LEAVING YOUR CLASSROOM, YOU SHOULD STIPU-
> LATE THE TYPE OF CONDUCT EXPECTED FROM THE STU-
> DENTS DURING YOUR ABSENCE. IN ADDITION, WHERE THE
> ABSENCE FROM THE CLASSROOM IS FOR AN UNREASON-
> ABLE AMOUNT OF TIME, YOU SHOULD *EXPECT* FORMS OF
> ROWDINESS, AND MUST THEREFORE TAKE PRECAU-
> TIONARY MEASURES TO ENSURE SAFETY.

Such a precautionary measure, for example, would be asking another teacher to check in on the students every few minutes. This in itself may not cover you. You should set down instructions to be followed in your absence, and you should take into consideration the students' age and actions of the past. For example, you would normally be all right in leaving 12 to 18-year olds alone for ten minutes. However, if the students were mentally retarded, known to be delinquent, or were too young to care for themselves in an ordinary classroom situation, leaving them might seem unreasonable. If you do not take the necessary precautions, you are putting yourself in unnecessary danger.

Ignorance:

Ignorance of a dangerous situation might cause you to be liable. The problem is in determining whether or not you are ignorant through your own fault, or if you had no reason or duty to be aware of a dangerous situation. Chemistry teachers should inspect dangerous chemicals and containers, and physical education teachers should inspect ropes that hang from the gym ceilings. Vocational teachers should inspect power tools at regular intervals, and if an elementary teacher sees broken glass on the playground, she should correct the danger.

You are also obligated to inform students of potentially dangerous conditions or activities. Before a student pole vaults into a sawdust pit, he should know some of the techniques of the skill, and he should be warned of the potential dangers. You should discuss the planned activities before the students begin participating in them. If you do this, you will generally be giving protection to yourself and to your students.

Forseeability:

If the consequences of an act are foreseeable, or should be foreseeable, you are liable for those consequences. For example:

GUIDE RULE
INJURY IS GENERALLY FORESEEABLE IN SITUATIONS (1) WHERE LARGE CROWDS OF STUDENTS ARE GATHERED WITHOUT SUPERVISION; (2) IN SPECIALIZED ACTIVITIES IN VOCATIONAL EDUCATION, PHYSICAL EDUCATION AND SCIENCE CLASSES; OR (3) IN CASES WHERE YOU ARE ABSENT FROM THE ROOM FOR AN UNREASONABLE AMOUNT OF TIME.

In a New Mexico case, an interesting, yet nearly tragic question of foreseeability became a major factor in a senior play. In this case, the injured student was an actress in a play that called for her to be shot by an actor with a gun shooting blank bullets. The blank shooting gun had been used previously, and was kept in the principal's office when not in use. The gun was not school property, but was the personal property of a student. However, the school took precautions in the use of the gun, and only those authorized were allowed to handle it. Prior to the last performance of the play, a student replaced the blank cartridge with a live bullet, and the girl was wounded. The injured student sued the one who exchanged the bullets, the director of the play, and the principal, alleging that the teacher and principal were negligent in their care of the pistol, and that they should have foreseen that her injury was a possible consequence of their lack of care. However, the court felt otherwise, and held that the degree of care on the part of the teacher and principal was that of the reasonable and prudent man in the same or similar circumstances, and that, since they were not negligent, no injury was foreseeable.[18] This is an interesting case, and could have gone either way. It is quite possible that the outcome could change by a mere change of location. For example, had the play been performed in a school district where violence had happened in the past, or where students in the play were known to play "tricks," there seems little doubt that the teacher and principal would be held to a higher degree of care, and should have been able to foresee that this type of injury could be inflicted.

WHEN CAN A TEACHER DEFEND NEGLIGENCE

Although you may be negligent in looking out for your student's safety, you should not be held responsible if his injury is due in part to his own negligence. Contributory negligence is the term given to this defense which is available to you. This defense is of limited utility, however. In most states, if a student is under the age of seven, the courts generally hold that he is incapable of contributory negligence. If the child is between the ages of seven and 14, the courts generally hold that he is presumed to be incapable of contributory negligence unless it can be shown otherwise. After age 14, the child is presumed capable of contributory negligence, but it must be proved. In states where these age stipulations are not followed exactly, the courts are nevertheless cognizant of their merit, and consider them as factors.

The concept of contributory negligence can best be illustrated by an example. Assume that you left your playground supervisory duty and permitted students to entertain themselves without any guidance. The students thought that it would be fun to walk the top of a fence around the playground. One student walked on top of the fence for ten minutes, but then slipped and fell to the ground, breaking his arm. (1) If the student was a six-year-old first grader, he could not legally be considered contributorily negligent. You would probably be considered negligent, and would be liable for the injuries the child suffered. (2) If the child involved were 12 years old, you could be considered negligent, but could try to prove that the child was also negligent. In other words, you could claim that your negligence was not the sole cause of the injury—in which case, you must prove that the child was capable of appreciating the possible danger, and was negligent by ignoring the danger. (3) If the student were 17, it would be fairly easy to prove contributory negligence.

Generally if the student is found to have been contributorily negligent in any substantial degree, you will not be liable for injuries sustained. This is true in most states, but there are various exceptions. In Wisconsin, Maine, Oregon, Nebraska, South Dakota, Arkansas and Mississippi, the law is more or less that a person is liable for the percentage of the injury that his act or omission caused. For example, Mississippi law is that if you were negligent, but the jury found that the student was ten per cent negligent, you would be liable for only 90 per cent of the damages. This concept (sometimes called "comparative negligence") is gaining in popularity, and may become law in many of the other states. The Texas Bar Association has recommended that this law be enacted everywhere, but, as yet, the law in Texas and in most states is that any contribution on the part of the injured party to his own injury precludes recovery, and frees the teacher from all liability.

Contributory negligence has saved teachers from liability in many cases, but it will not save you if the student was following instructions.

GUIDE RULE	IN CASES WHERE THE STUDENT IS DIRECTED BY THE TEACHER TO DO SOMETHING, AND THE STUDENT IS INJURED, THE COURTS HAVE UNIFORMLY HELD THAT THE CHILD IS NOT NEGLIGENT NO MATTER WHAT HIS AGE.

For example, if a physical education instructor directed a child with extremely weak wrists to climb the rope to the top of the gymnasium, the teacher could be found negligent if he was aware of the child's weakness. He could not defend on the grounds that the student contributed to his own injury by letting go of the rope, because the student was following instructions.

SUMMARY

If you are ever involved in a lawsuit with one of your students, there is a good chance that the case will involve negligence. The student will try to prove that you had a duty of caring for his safety, and you failed in carrying out that duty. On the other hand, you will need to prove that your action, or lack of action, was reasonable under the circumstances.

Because you work with so many students, and because there are so many different activities, you must make certain that you act in the way a prudent teacher would act in the same circumstances. The prudent teacher will take into consideration such things as age of students, general maturity, the possibility of injury, and the supervision required for safety. If you consider these factors before you engage in an activity, you will generally be able to avoid negligent injuries.

Rules and regulations play an important part in preventing accidents. Because you are responsible for safety, you may make rules and regulations which are necessary safety precautions. The rules and regulations must be clearly communicated to your students, and must be enforced.

You are not expected to be everywhere at all times, but you are expected to reasonably supervise student activities. This supervisory duty can be delegated to others only where the delegation is reasonable under the circumstances, and where the other person is responsible enough to handle the situation. You must exercise a higher standard of care over your students than the ordinary man in the street. You must act as the "ordinary" teacher. This means that you should be careful in delegating your responsibilities to students within your classroom, or to someone who is not trained in caring for children. The essence of negligence is the lack of properly caring for children in a way that would normally be expected. This is your responsibility, and must be given careful consideration at all times.

Some injuries can be anticipated. If circumstances are such that you should anticipate an injury, you are under the duty to act in alleviating the condition. A wrongful act might be considered negligence. Also, neglecting to act where you should can be considered negligence. Where there are large gatherings of students, and where your students are left for an unreasonable amount of time, accidents are easier to foresee. Precautionary measures should therefore be taken before someone is injured.

Some teaching positions have a higher risk involved when talking about negligent accidents. Physical education teachers, science teachers, vocational instructors and elementary teachers should be especially aware of their added responsibility. In addition, almost all teachers are given supervisory duties during lunch periods, recess, or assemblies. These duties must be taken seriously. Preventing an accident can prevent a lawsuit. More important, a safe environment will make your duties easier to fulfill, and your job more enjoyable.

FOOTNOTES

1 Morris v. Douglas County School Dist., 403 P.2d 775 (Ore. 1965).
2 State v. Board of Education, 23 N.W. 102, 103 (Wis. 1885).
3 Cioffi v. Board of Education of City of New York, 278 N.Y.S. 2d 249 (Sup. Ct., App.D., N.Y. 1967).
4 Lawes v. Board of Education of City of New York, 213 N.E. 2d 667, 668 (Ct. of App., N.Y. 1965).
5 Hoose v. Drumm, 22 N.E. 2d 233, 234 (Ct. of App., N.Y. 1939).
6 Selleck v. Board of Education, 94 N.Y.S. 2d 318, 276 App. Div. 263 (N.Y. 1949).
7 Titus v. Lindberg, 228 A. 2d 65, 68 (N.J. 1967).
8 Engle v. Gosper, 177 A.2d 595 (N.J. 1962).
9 Govel v. Board of Education of City of Albany, 48 N.Y.S.2d 299, 267 App. Div. 621 (N.Y. 1944).
10 Guerriere v. Tyson, 24 A.2d 468 (Pa. 1942).
11 Bellman v. San Francisco High School District, 11 Cal. 2d 576, 81 P.2d 894 (Cal. 1939).
12 Ibid.
13 Berry v. Arnold School District, 137 S.W.2d 256 (Ark. 1940).
14 Verduce v. Board of Higher Education of City of New York, 168 N.E.2d 838 (Ct. of App., N.Y. 1960).
15 Holmes, O.W. Jr., *The Common Law*, Little Brown & Company, Boston, Mass., p. 108, 1881.
16 Garber v. Central School District No.I, 295 N.Y.S. 850, 251 App. Div. 214 (N.Y. 1937).
17 Ohman v. Board of Education of City of New York, 88 N.Y.S.2d 273, 275 App. Div. 840 (N.Y. 1949).
18 Ferreira v. Sanchez, 449 P2d 784 (N. Mex. 1969).

FOUR

Preserving the Constitutional Rights of Teachers

In medieval England, people believed that the laws of nature, the "natural law," would provide the solution to man's problems. In deciding many cases, the courts sought to discover what the laws of nature were. Emerging from these decisions were principles which became known as the "common law." The common law of England formed the basis for the original law of the United States, and today, many of the laws which govern the operations of the public schools and teachers exist because of the common law. The common law is based on court decisions, not on legislative enactments.

The other major source of law is the Constitution of the United States. This is the "supreme law of the land." All laws passed by Congress or state legislatures, ordinances passed by cities or other local governmental bodies, and rules and regulations set up by boards of education are subject to the provisions of the Constitution. The Constitution sets forth much of the basic law which governs state and federal agencies, but it does not specifically refer to education. Therefore, education is primarily a matter for the individual states, and most laws affecting you and your school system can be found in the statutes passed by your state legislatures. On the other hand, the Constitution specifically protects certain individual rights guaranteed to every citizen. As a result, no laws, ordinances or rules or regulations may restrict you from exercising those personal rights which are granted by the Constitution.

Most private employers have the right to hire and fire their employees for whatever reasons they choose. Unlike the school board, these employers are not generally governed by the provisions of the Constitution. Since education is a state function, the state is the employer of public school teachers. The school board acts as an agent for the state. The state cannot enact a law which is inconsistent with the Constitution. Therefore, any rule or regulation enacted by the school board which substantially infringes on your constitutional rights is invalid. The First Amendment provides that individuals have the right to freedom of speech and assembly. This means that:

1. You have a right to speak freely outside the classroom.
2. You have the right to speak freely within the classroom.
3. You may express yourself through your personal appearance.
4. Your private life is of little concern to the school board.
5. You may engage in "civil rights" activities, and associate with the friends of your own choice.
6. You cannot be dismissed, suspended, or subjected to any other form of disciplinary action for exercising your constitutional rights.

These rights, however, are not absolute. As an employer, the state has the right to enact *reasonable* rules and regulations in order to promote the efficient operation and necessary discipline of its schools. Some of these rules and regulations may incidentally curtail your constitutional rights to a limited extent. There are guidelines which will help you to determine if these curtailments are valid. The courts will balance your protected rights with the protected rights of the school board. Keep in mind that the courts will favor your rights because they are specifically provided for by the Constitution. This chapter includes guide rules and cases that represent the factors which will be considered in the balancing of your rights against your employer's.

Although you will find that you have many more rights than you thought, consider carefully that there are times when it is not wise to exercise them. There are many advantages in getting along with the school board, your supervisors and colleagues. Their help and cooperation is often necessary in order for you to function to your fullest capacity and effectiveness. You have a desire and a duty to provide your students with the best possible education. Sometimes this will call for you to exercise your rights, but there may be times when they will benefit more if you do not exercise them. Either way, you cannot be punished for doing or not doing so.

YOUR FREEDOM OF SPEECH OUTSIDE THE CLASSROOM

When you are outside of the school building, you often discuss the topics which are of interest and concern to you as an individual and not as a teacher Some of these discussions involve controversial subjects, and you may wonder if your statements can ever form the basis for dismissal from your teaching duties. In the past, two main reasons were given for allowing teachers to be dismissed because of their extramural statements. The first reason was that the statements might bring discredit to the school. The second reason was that the statements could reflect on the teacher's fitness.

The first argument might be valid in a situation where the school's financing relies on private contributions from the public; however, it is of questionable relevance for public elementary and secondary schools. The second argument is much stronger. Statements may either render the teacher incapable of fulfilling his duties, or may indicate that the teacher will use the classroom as a forum for advocating objectionable views. This has often come up in cases where the teacher is admittedly a Communist. Some of the more important factors which need to be considered in judging whether or not the statements are an indication of unfitness are:

1. The level of education.
2. The subject which is taught.
3. The nature of the statement.

Courts of the past allowed a teacher to be dismissed merely if his statements *indicated* he was unfit to teach. A *clear demonstration* of unfitness was not required. The reason for this is that these courts did not recognize the teacher's right to freedom of speech. In a case arising during the Second World War, a Florida court upheld the dismissal of a teacher who had publicly stated that he was a conscientious objector and would not aid the United States as a combatant or non-combatant. Although the teacher had been in the Florida public schools for ten years, and was admittedly conscientious, experienced and well-qualified professionally, the court said that he was incompetent because he was incapable of teaching his students honesty and patriotism by precept and example. They said that the true test of patriotism could be measured by the willingness of the teacher to bear arms and defend his country.[1]

In another World War II case, a high school history teacher from Illinois was dismissed for what was termed "conduct unbecoming a teacher." Here, the teacher had written a letter to a former student who refused to register for the draft, congratulating him on his "courageous and idealistic stand." She also wished him success, saying that "you and the others who take the same stand are the hope of America." The court upheld the dismissal and said that the teacher's action would undermine the morale of the young military-aged men in her classes, and would encourage them to violate the law. The court felt that this was not a proper patriotic attitude for a teacher to display.[2]

The teachers in these cases were clearly denied a right of free speech. Decisions such as these were based on the public's interest in preserving the integrity of its schools and in protecting children from incompetent teachers.

This interest is unquestioned. However, free and unhindered debate on matters of public importance is also a desirable goal, and it must be fully considered if a proper balance is to be struck. Society's interest in encouraging such debate is so great that in the 1968 case of *Pickering v. Board of Education,*[3] the United States Supreme Court said:

GUIDE RULE

... ABSENT PROOF OF FALSE STATEMENTS KNOWINGLY OR RECKLESSLY MADE BY HIM, A TEACHER'S EXERCISE OF HIS RIGHT TO SPEAK ON ISSUES OF PUBLIC IMPORTANCE MAY NOT FURNISH THE BASIS FOR HIS DISMISSAL FROM PUBLIC EMPLOYMENT.

This case has become the most important, precise and controlling decision on the right of a teacher to speak freely outside the classroom. The teacher in this case had written a letter to a local newspaper criticizing the way the board of education and the superintendent handled proposals to raise revenue. In the letter, he said that (1) the school board misinformed the public about the allocation of finances in a proposed school bond issue; and (2) the school superintendent threatened to discipline any teacher who refused to support the school bond. The school board dismissed the teacher on the grounds that the publication was detrimental to the efficient operation of the schools. The Supreme Court saw through this argument, and upheld Pickering's claim that the dismissal denied him his First Amendment rights. The Court said that teachers may not constitutionally be compelled to relinquish their right to comment on matters of public interest concerning the operation of the public schools. The reasoning behind this decision is that:

> Teachers are, as a class, the members of a community most likely to have informed and definite opinions as to how funds allotted to the operation of the schools should be spent. Accordingly, it is essential that they be able to speak out freely on such questions without fear of retaliatory dismissal.[4]

The Court, in *Pickering,* recognized that the threat of dismissal is a potent means of inhibiting speech. Therefore:

GUIDE RULE

BEFORE YOUR OUT-OF-CLASS SPEECH MAY BE RESTRICTED, THERE MUST BE A SHOWING THAT YOUR UTTERANCES HARM A *SUBSTANTIAL* PUBLIC INTEREST OR RENDER YOU UNFIT TO TEACH.

Deciding what a "substantial public interest" is, and when it has been harmed, has often been a difficult problem. However, the Supreme Court in deciding Pickering's case provided some of the more important factors that should be considered in analyzing the effect of the teacher's words:

	1. Disruption of superior-subordinate relationships;
Pickering	2. Breach of loyalty or confidentiality;
Standards	3. General disruption of the public service;
to	4. Indication of unfitness from content of the statement;
Consider	and
	5. Failure to comply with established grievance procedures.

These factors will no doubt form the basis for future decisions. The courts will look at these factors to judge whether or not your statements are harmful to a substantial public interest. An examination of cases decided subsequent to *Pickering* may help to point out how the courts are going to apply these standards.

In a case arising in New York, a high school teacher was suspended without pay for "conduct unbecoming a teacher" and "insubordination." He had distributed a letter to teachers and administrators in the school district. The letter contained several factual inaccuracies, and criticized, in no uncertain terms, the school board's failure to renew the contract of a probationary teacher. The court found that the teacher should not have been suspended. They reasoned that the teacher's indiscretions led to no deleterious effects within the school system, and it was unlikely that they should have. The court said that indiscreet bombast, to the limited extent of this letter, could not sustain disciplinary action. Otherwise, teachers would be discouraged from exercising their right to speak on issues of public importance, or would be forced to couch their criticisms in mild, ineffective terms.[5] This case supports the general rule that:

1. You have the right to criticize the school board or superintendent.
2. You can comment freely on the school budget or on the school system in general.
3. If you feel that one of your fellow teachers, or students, has been treated unfairly, you cannot be disciplined for saying so.

You may exercise these rights freely, but hopefully you will do so in the name of academic freedom and in the best interests of your school. Calling people names or criticizing them excessively cannot help but have some ill effects. You may win your lawsuit, but still feel that you are in danger of being later considered unfit or incompetent. No doubt your teaching methods and materials will be watched carefully; this cannot be helped. Consider all of the possible effects your criticism will have. Ask yourself to what extent your criticism will help improve your educational system, and even more importantly, will your students benefit in the long run. You have the right to criticize constructively, but there are times when you and your students will benefit more if you do not do so. The only legal limitations on these rights are brought out in the following two cases.

In 1969, a California court permitted teachers to circulate a petition critical of the state legislature on school premises during duty-free lunch periods.[6] The petition, opposing reductions in the legislature's proposed budget, was controversial and critical, and therefore, was bound to create some disharmony within the school district. But the court held that the danger justifying restriction or prohibition must be one which is much greater than "public inconvenience, annoyance or unrest . . . ."

<table>
<tr><td>**GUIDE**
RULE</td><td>THERE MUST BE A SUBSTANTIAL THREAT TO THE ORDER AND EFFICIENCY OF THE SCHOOL SYSTEM TO JUSTIFY A LIMITATION ON YOUR FREEDOM OF SPEECH OUTSIDE THE CLASSROOM.</td></tr>
</table>

Therefore, if it is clear that your statements will substantially disrupt the public service, you would be wise not to make such criticisms. Some disharmony and unhappiness with your criticism is to be expected, however, and must be tolerated by the school board.

In Alaska, two tenured teachers were discharged for having compiled, reproduced and distributed an open letter which was critical of the school superintendent. The court upheld the dismissal of the teachers by applying the *Pickering* standards.[7] They found that (1) the superintendent was the immediate superior of the teachers in this relatively small Alaskan school district, and the statements, some of which were false, were detrimental to the harmony and discipline in the operation of the schools; (2) the criticisms aimed at the superintendent were more in the nature of personal grievances, rather than matters of legitimate public concern; and, (3) the false statements contained in the letter reflected on the integrity and ability of the superintendent and were not made in good faith. When combined, these facts and circumstances constituted sufficient reasons for a valid discharge.

In view of the problems presented in this case, the Alaska legislature amended the state statute dealing with permissible reasons for dismissal of teachers:

> No bylaw or regulation of the commissioner of education, a school board, or local school administrator may restrict or modify the right of a teacher to engage in comment and criticism outside school hours, regarding school personnel, members of the governing body of any school or school district, any other public official, or any school employee, to the same extent that any private individual may exercise the right.[8]

Thus, by statute, Alaska recognizes that teachers have the full privileges freedom of expression provides. Even so, in view of the disruption of the superior-subordinate relationship, and disruption of the discipline and harmony in the schools, the teachers in the prior case were properly dismissed. This stands for the proposition that you should not knowingly make false statements or publicly criticize your *immediate* superior. To do so would undermine close-working relationships and confidentiality. If you have a complaint to make about your immediate supervisor, you must follow the school's established grievance procedures. This also prevents personal problems from creating publicity which is detrimental to the school system.

When the teacher's extramural utterances call into question his fitness to teach, the statements may be an indication of general unfitness. This is particularly true in cases involving non-tenured teachers, because the school board is justified in observing him and evaluating his responses in public discussions during his probationary period. Although he has a right of free speech, his style may raise doubts as to the quality of his fitness for the position. Nevertheless, the school board must clearly prove that the teacher is unfit before they can dismiss him. This requires more than a mere showing of the statement alone. The school board must, for example, show that the statements have rendered the teacher unfit to teach by causing him to lose the respect and discipline of his students.

GUIDE RULE	EVEN THOUGH YOUR UTTERANCES MAY BE EVIDENCE OF GENERAL UNFITNESS, THEY MAY NOT ALONE CONSTITUTE AN INDEPENDENT BASIS FOR DISMISSAL.

The final standard suggested by the *Pickering* case, failure to comply with established grievance procedures, has not been involved in many court cases. If your criticism of school officials or the school system is based merely on internal matters, such as the selection of textbooks, or working conditions, you are expected to exhaust internal grievance procedures before making the grievance public. Disciplinary action might be appropriate in some instances where you have failed to do so. Two difficulties with such procedures are obvious: (1) An employee cannot be deemed properly discharged for insubordination when the school's grievance procedures are buried deep in an employee handbook or are written in obscure language and have not been made known to him; and (2) often such procedures force the employee to take his complaint directly to the person about whom he is complaining. Courts recognize this, and will consider these factors if you have failed to comply with established grievance procedures.

YOUR FREEDOM OF SPEECH WITHIN THE CLASSROOM

Constitutional freedoms must be vigilantly protected in the classrooms of American schools. You and your students must be free to work in an atmosphere which is conducive to stimulating curiosity, questioning old and new concepts, and searching for self identity. To attain a high standard of education requires academic freedom. The intellectual leaders of our public schools and colleges must be free from rigid requirements of standardization and conformity. Academic freedom has been recognized by the courts as an interest they will endeavor to protect. As the United States Supreme Court has said:

> Our nation is deeply committed to safeguarding academic freedom, which is of transcendent value to all of us and not merely to the teachers concerned. That freedom is therefore a special concern of the First Amendment, which does not tolerate laws that cast a pall of orthodoxy over the classroom.[9]

American people over the years traditionally believed that the function of schools was the transmission rather than the discovery of knowledge. As a result, many people suggested that free speech and academic freedom were of questionable relevance in public elementary or secondary classrooms. They felt that, since the word of the teacher may carry great authority, the assumption of "the marketplace of ideas" was not applicable. This line of thinking was derived in part from cases such as that of the famed "monkey trial."[10]

In this celebrated case, the court upheld the conviction of John Scopes, a biology teacher. He had been charged with violating Tennessee's "monkey law." This "anti-evolution" statute essentially made it unlawful for a teacher in any state-supported school "to teach any theory that denies the story of the divine creation of man as taught in the Bible, and to teach instead that man has descended from a lower order of animals." Even the eloquent advocacy of Clarence Darrow was unable to convince the court that the statute was unconstitutional. Scopes was dismissed and fined one hundred dollars.

In 1967, Tennessee finally repealed its "monkey law," and by 1968, Arkansas and Mississippi were the only states having anti-evolution statutes. A young, tenth-grade biology teacher in Little Rock, Arkansas, wanted to use a book in her classes which taught the Darwinian theory. She therefore instituted a suit to have the anti-evolution statute declared unconstitutional. The Supreme Court of the United States ruled that states have the right to prescribe the curriculum for its schools, but they do not have the right to prohibit the teaching of a scientific theory or doctrine where the prohibition is based on reasons that violate freedoms of speech and religion.[11]

How does this affect you? The change in society's philosophy toward the concept of schools is somewhat apparent when comparing the "monkey trial" of the 1920's and the Arkansas case of the 1960's. In the first decision, it was felt that censorship of disagreeable philosophies was within the state's rights. However, by the time of the Arkansas decision, it was felt that the state could no longer make it a criminal offense for a public school teacher to mention the existence of a different school of respected human thought. The grade level is an important factor to be considered in judging the appropriateness of the teacher's statements, but it is not the sole consideration. Modernly, there is a recognition of the need for some academic freedom at all levels of education.

Nevertheless, not all of the recent decisions have been unanimous in recognizing this need. In one case, the court upheld a school board's failure to renew the contract of a non-tenured teacher who had assigned Aldous Huxley's book, *Brave New World,* in violation of school regulations.[12] This decision was not in line with modern judicial thought, and is contrary to the majority rule. Rigorous censorship, the United States Supreme Court says, has the "unmistakable tendency to chill that free play of the spirit which all teachers ought especially to cultivate and practice."[13] The case involving *Brave New World* appears to have ignored this. The reasoning of a subsequent decision dealing with academic freedom is more in tune with the thoughts and needs of our time. In holding that a teacher could not be suspended for having assigned a non-pornographic scholarly article to his senior English class, even though the article contained some vulgar and offensive language, the court said:

> If the answer were that the students must be protected from such exposure, we would fear for their future. We do not question the good faith of the defendants in believing that some parents have been offended. With the greatest of respect to such parents, their sensibilities are not the full measure of what is proper education.[14]

The court is suggesting that, to maintain an atmosphere of academic freedom, school boards and parents should not be allowed to base regulations of free speech on their own personal opinions. This is not to say that you may present any and all materials to your class, but:

<table>
<tr><td>GUIDE
RULE</td><td>YOU HAVE A RIGHT TO PRESENT SCHOLARLY, NON-PORNOGRAPHIC MATERIAL TO YOUR CLASS. CENSORSHIP OF SUCH MATERIAL BASED MERELY ON THE OPINIONS OF A FEW PARENTS WILL NOT BE ALLOWED.</td></tr>
</table>

As a result of the many decisions extending the teacher's First Amendment freedoms, you are free to discuss controversial topics, ideas and philosophies in the classroom which relate to your particular subject. Thus, in another case, it was found that a social science teacher could not be dismissed for supporting student demands for greater campus freedom during her classroom lectures, because the school's operation was not substantially impaired.[15] However, there have been cases where students have gotten so aroused through such discussions that they are actually ready to riot. You have a duty to present both sides of any controversy, and should try to calculate the discussion's potential effect. You cannot be held responsible for a completely unforeseeable result, but if your discussions reasonably will lead to disruption of the educational process, or to student violence, your speech is not constitutionally protected. Also:

GUIDE RULE   IF THE TEACHER CLEARLY USES THE CLASSROOM MERELY AS A FORUM TO ESPOUSE HIS PERSONAL POLITICAL VIEWS WHICH ARE COMPLETELY IRRELEVANT TO THE SUBJECT BEING TAUGHT, HE MAY RIGHTFULLY BE DISMISSED.

This point is illustrated by a case in which the teacher, acting as a civilian employee for the Air Force, taught basic English to foreign military officers who were in this country as guests of the U.S. government. He had been warned that discussion of controversial topics was contrary to Air Force policy. Nevertheless, on one occasion, the teacher told his class that those who burned themselves to death to protest the Vietnam war were the true heroes, and he wished that he had the courage to do so himself. On another occasion, he told his class that the Jewish people were discriminated against in the United States, and that he personally had experienced such discrimination throughout his life. The language of the court best describes their reasons for upholding the dismissal:

> On the record before us, we must assume that appellant [meaning the teacher] was fired for what he said *within* the classroom to foreign officers who were supposed to be learning how to cope with an English-speaking dentist or garage repairman, and not for airing his views outside the classroom to anyone who would listen. There is nothing to suggest that appellant was required to keep his opinions to himself at all times or under all circumstances, but only in the immediate context of his highly specialized teaching assignment—and we stress the uniqueness of appellant's teaching function in our disposition of this point. In view of that uniqueness, we cannot say that any of the interests underlying the First Amendment were served by the appellant's insistence upon intruding his personal views into the classroom, or

that his employer was disabled by those interests from imposing and enforcing the very limited restriction emerging from this record.[16]

As you can see, the court was concerned mainly about the complete absence of relevance the comments had to the subject being taught, and the specialized area of the teaching assignment. What you say should be relevant to the subject you teach, and within the student's capability to understand, in order for your speech to be fully protected. In other words, you can discuss controversial public matter more freely in a "social studies" class than in a mathematics class. You can also be more free in your discussions with high school students than with elementary students.

Lending further support to the argument that academic freedom exists at all levels of education is an Iowa case involving students. Several students who wore black armbands to school as a means of protesting the Vietnam war were sent home and told not to return until they removed the armbands. The United States Supreme Court said that the school board regulation prohibiting the wearing of black armbands to school was unconstitutional. The Court said that the wearing of symbols of political or controversial significance by high school students, in circumstances which are not conducive to potentially disruptive conduct, is constitutionally protected free speech.[17] Although no teachers were involved, the court clearly indicated that the principles set forth were equally applicable to teachers as well as students.

The Supreme Court applied a test which suggests that prohibitions or restrictions on speech should only be permitted where it can be shown that such utterances "materially and substantially interfere with the requirements of appropriate discipline in the operation of the school." This test was adopted from an earlier decision, which held that a prohibition against the wearing of freedom buttons was unconstitutional, absent such a showing of interference.[18]

GUIDE RULE YOUR FREEDOM OF SPEECH MAY BE RESTRICTED ONLY WHERE IT MATERIALLY AND SUBSTANTIALLY INTERFERES WITH THE REQUIREMENTS OF APPROPRIATE DISCIPLINE IN THE OPERATION OF THE SCHOOL.

Where harassment or actual disruption of the educational process is shown, such prohibitions will be upheld, however. What is appropriate discipline will of course vary with the individual facts and circumstances.

In the armband case, the Court recognized that when controversial ideas are expressed, unrest is inevitable but tolerance is required, even in the schools. The Court said:

Any word spoken, in class, in the lunchroom, or on the campus, that deviates from the views of another person may start an argument or cause a disturbance. But our Constitution says we must take this risk . . . .

In order for . . . school officials to justify prohibition of a particular expression . . . [they] must be able to show that [their] action was caused by something more than a mere desire to avoid the discomfort and unpleasantness that always accompany an unpopular viewpoint.[19]

This means that you are allowed to discuss controversial ideas in your class, even though some unpleasantness or minor disruption may result. You have a duty to care about all of your students, however, and you should try to control the discussions, in an effort to avoid personal attacks or undue hurt feelings to any of your students.

Free and open discussion of controversial topics is essential, for the classroom is the "marketplace of ideas." Students necessarily must be exposed to a variety of ideas from which they may form and discover their own conception of truth. For this reason, academic freedom exists at all levels of education, and your freedom of speech within the classroom is to a great extent protected.

YOUR PERSONAL APPEARANCE AS AN EXPRESSION OF YOUR PERSONALITY, HERITAGE, RACE OR CULTURE

The courts have shown an increasing willingness to scrutinize school board regulations on teacher dress and personal appearance. You are aware that your appearance is of some importance in building your image and respect among the students and the community. But can it be said that a mustache, beard, or pants suit detracts from an otherwise "clean cut" appearance?

In a case arising in Pasadena, California, it was decided that a teacher could not be removed from his regular classroom duties because he wore a beard. The high school teacher had not been dismissed, but was transferred to home teaching. The court ordered him reinstated, and said that: "[T]he wearing of a beard is a form of expression of an individual's personality."[20] The court went on to say that:

> [W]ith the complete absence of any actual experience at the high school involved as to what the actual adverse effect of the wearing of a beard by a male teacher would be upon the conduct of the educational processes there, beards as such, without regard to their general appearance, their neatness and their cleanliness cannot constitutionally be banned from the classroom and from the campus.[21]

There was no showing by the principal or the superintendent of any actual adverse effect that the beard would have upon the educational system. As the court suggested, if such a showing had been made, the result of the case might have been different.

During the Christmas vacation of 1968-1969, a teacher in Massachusetts grew a neat, short, well-trimmed beard. When he returned to school, he was informed by the principal that it was the unwritten policy that teachers be clean shaven. The teacher refused to shave, and he was subsequently suspended without having been given a full hearing. The school district was ordered to reinstate the teacher with back pay, and to give him one thousand dollars for his pain and suffering. The question as to whether the teacher had a constitutionally protected right to wear a beard was not directly answered, but the court did find that freedom to wear a beard was ". . . an interest of his, especially in combination with his professional reputation as a school teacher, which may not be taken from him without due process of law."[22]

Another case involved a superior French teacher in Florida who was the only black teacher on a 110-member faculty. This teacher refused to comply with the request of the principal that he remove his goatee. No written rule or established policy existed within the school district as to the discretion conferred on each principal relative to personal appearance. Also, there was no showing that the wearing of the goatee by the teacher might reasonably be expected to, or did, in fact, cause disruption of pupil discipline or the educational process at the school. The court ruled that the wearing of a beard by a teacher is a constitutionally protected liberty, and said that, "Furthermore, where, as here, it is worn as 'an appropriate expression of his heritage, culture and racial pride as a black man,' its wearer also enjoys the protection of first amendment rights."[23] In this case, the court found that, under the circumstances, the principal's request was arbitrary, unreasonable, and based on personal preference. The court ordered the school board to reappoint the teacher.

Cases involving student appearance lend further support to the proposition that school boards may not impose rigid, unreasonable standards of appearance on teachers. The modern trend of judicial reasoning is perhaps best expressed in a statement made by a federal judge referring to a high school regulation limiting the length of hair:

> I pray to God that in these United States we do not judge a man by the length of his hair or the clothes he wears but rather we try to evaluate him on his humanity, his personality. Even Jesus Christ couldn't go to your high school. Neither could the twelve apostles.[24]

Although it is assumed that the courts are going to base their decisions involving teachers' personal appearance on whether or not there is a clear demonstration of actual or potential impairment of the educational process, it is still too early to say for certain what the result will be under the varied circumstances. This is because there is no controlling United States Supreme Court decision. Many courts will probably say that:

GUIDE **RULE**	IF YOUR APPEARANCE IS AN EXPRESSION OF YOUR PER- SONALITY, HERITAGE, RACE OR CULTURE, AND IT DOES NOT IMPAIR THE EDUCATIONAL PROCESS, YOU ARE PRO- TECTED UNDER THE CONSTITUTION.

However, it is possible that some courts might say your appearance is not an expression of speech at all, and therefore, will not be protected by the First Amendment. In view of the fact that the law in this area is changing rapidly, and varies greatly from state to state, it must be recommended that if you are asked to shave, cut your hair, or otherwise comply with appearance regulations, you either do so or consult an attorney before you refuse.

How a person is dressed and looks often affects the way he acts. Being able to express yourself through your appearance may help you to relate to your students. They are able to see you as you really are, and many teachers find that this helps them in developing a sense of rapport with their students. But do not let your desire to express yourself get in the way of your teaching effectiveness. Wearing a see-through blouse with no bra, as one teacher did, would make it rather difficult for many students to concentrate. Hot pants are rather distracting, too. This type of dress cannot be allowed, because it impairs the teaching process. Restrictions on this type of dress are therefore legally permissible.

HOW YOUR PRIVATE LIFE AFFECTS YOUR EMPLOYMENT

The standards set forth in the *Pickering* case have lent support to the argument that your private *conduct* may be grounds for dismissal only where it affects your fitness as a teacher. Prior to the mid-1960's, the courts had upheld teacher dismissals based on a wide variety of private conduct not directly related to their fitness as teachers. For example, in one instance, the dismissal of a teacher who had been drinking beer, playing a pinball machine, and shaking dice for drinks in a public restaurant in front of students, was upheld.[25]

In 1967, an Ohio court said that a teacher could not be dismissed for "immorality" merely for writing a private letter containing language some people might find vulgar and offensive. In this instance, they said:

GUIDE
RULE

THE PRIVATE CONDUCT OF A MAN, WHO IS ALSO A
TEACHER, IS A PROPER CONCERN TO THOSE WHO EMPLOY
HIM ONLY TO THE EXTENT IT MARS HIM AS A TEACHER
... WHERE HIS PROFESSIONAL ACHIEVEMENT IS UNAF-
FECTED, WHERE THE SCHOOL COMMUNITY IS PLACED IN
NO JEOPARDY, HIS PRIVATE ACTS ARE HIS OWN BUSINESS
AND MAY NOT BE THE BASIS OF DISCIPLINE.[26]

This approach was also applied in a later Ohio case, in which the court ruled
that a teacher could not be dismissed for "immorality" merely because he
had been convicted of "hit and run" driving.[27]

California's highest court has also applied the "fitness as a teacher" test.
It said that a teacher who had engaged in a limited non-criminal homosexual
relationship could not have his teaching certificate revoked. The court did
not say that homosexuals must be permitted to teach in the public schools,
but it did say that they can be prohibited only if it is shown that they are
unfit.[28] In discussing the fitness test, the court said:

> In determining whether the teacher's conduct thus indicates unfitness to
> teach the board may consider such matters as the likelihood that the conduct
> may have adversely affected students or fellow teachers, the degree of such
> adversity anticipated, the proximity or remoteness in time of the conduct,
> the type of teaching certificate held by the party involved, the extenuating or
> aggravating circumstances, if any, surrounding the conduct, the praiseworthi-
> ness or blameworthiness of the motives resulting in the conduct, the
> likelihood of the reoccurrence of the questioned conduct, and the extent to
> which disciplinary action may inflict an adverse impact or chilling effect upon
> the constitutional rights of the teacher involved or other teachers. These
> factors are relevant to the extent that they assist the board in determining a
> teacher's fitness to teach.[29]

These cases point out that there is an increasing desire by the courts to
protect your private life. You should not feel that you must set an example
for the community. Your actions, habits and life style are of no concern to
your employer, so long as you are fit to teach.

One report demonstrated how educators differed in their opinions as to
whether dismissal for "unprofessional conduct" might include "imbibing
alcoholic beverages, use of tobacco, signing petitions, revealing contents of
school documents to legislative committees, appealing directly to one's
legislative representative, and opposing major opinions."[30] Teachers must be
protected from being dismissed because of their administrator's personal bias
or opinions. The most valid, uniform test to apply to your personal conduct
is that test which requires a showing of unfitness to teach.

YOUR FREEDOM TO ORGANIZE AND ASSOCIATE
WITH THE FRIENDS OF YOUR CHOICE

The First Amendment says that you have the right to assemble peaceably. Aside from its literal meaning, it protects your right to associate with the people or groups of your choice. Therefore, you may not be punished in any way for belonging to a union. Most of the problems arising in this area involve political activity and "subversive" organizations.

Traditionally, restrictions have been imposed on teachers' freedom to engage in political activity. Today, these restrictions no longer exist for most purposes. Where state laws attempt to forbid public employees from participating in *any* form of political activity, the laws have been invalidated. Some decisions suggest that *non-partisan* political activity does not affect the teacher's fitness or classroom performance, and therefore, this activity may not be restricted. However, where *partisan* political activity is concerned, the courts have not consistently or clearly stated their position.

In the past, the courts felt that the state's interests were paramount to the right of public employees to engage in partisan political activity. Laws which prohibited federal civil service employees from participating in political management or political campaigns were considered valid. The validity of this position is now in serious doubt. More recent cases suggest that laws prohibiting civil service employees from holding or running for public office, or participating in any political campaigns, are unconstitutional restrictions of First Amendment rights. A standard which future decisions will probably follow was suggested by a 1969 case involving a teacher in Alaska.[31]

GUIDE **RULE**	POLITICAL ACTIVITY WHICH MATERIALLY AND SUBSTANTIALLY INTERFERES WITH THE EFFICIENCY AND DISCIPLINE IN THE OPERATION OF THE SCHOOL MAY PROPERLY BE RESTRICTED; BUT ABSENT SUCH INTERFERENCE, YOUR RIGHT TO PARTICIPATE IN POLITICAL ACTIVITIES MAY NOT BE RESTRICTED.

You have a right to participate in civil rights activities, and therefore, you may not be refused re-employment, suspended or subjected to any other sanctions for exercising this right. In a South Carolina case, it was decided that the school board abused its discretion in terminating the employment of a teacher because he participated in civil rights demonstrations. The court said:

> So that no public school teacher may be deprived of those personal liberties secured by the United States Constitution the discretion exercised by

the school boards must be within reasonable limits, so as not to curtail, impinge or infringe upon the freedom of political expression or association, or any other constitutionally protected rights.[32]

As a result, you should feel free to express your political or social concerns. You have the right to belong to various political or civil rights groups, and you may engage in their legal activities without fearing reprisal by your employer.

Restraints on the right of public employees to organize are unconstitutional. Regardless of its aims or objectives, you have the right to belong to any organization you desire. In New York, three instructors at the State University of New York each refused to sign a certificate that he was not a Communist, and that if he had ever been a Communist, he had communicated that fact to the president of the university. The teachers were notified that their refusal to sign the loyalty oath violated a New York law, and therefore, they would be dismissed. They still refused to sign. Harry Keyishian's contract was not renewed, and he appealed to the courts. The United States Supreme Court invalidated the part of the law which provided for the removal of any teacher who belonged to any organization which advocated unlawful overthrow of the government.[33]

The Supreme Court said that the state must rely on affirmative actions by the teacher, or show other evidence of the teacher's illegal intent.

GUIDE RULE	MERE MEMBERSHIP IN A SUBVERSIVE ORGANIZATION IS NOT ENOUGH TO JUSTIFY DISMISSAL OR OTHER NON-CRIMINAL SANCTIONS. YOU MUST BE SHOWN TO HAVE THE INTENT TO BRING ABOUT THE ILLEGAL OBJECTIVES OF THE ORGANIZATION.

The reasoning behind this is found in another case in which Arizona's loyalty oath was challenged by a teacher. There, the Supreme Court said:

> Those who join an organization but do not share its unlawful purposes and who do not participate in its unlawful activities surely pose no threat, either as citizens or as public employees. Laws such as this which are not restricted in scope to those who join with the "specific intent" to further illegal action impose, in effect, a conclusive presumption that the member shares the unlawful aims of the organization.[34]

This is not to say that all loyalty oaths are invalid. You should be willing to sign an oath that you do not have the specific intent to aid in an unlawful attempt to overthrow the government of the United States.

"Guilt by association" cannot and should not be permitted. Mr. Justice William O. Douglas was concerned about teachers and academic freedom as long ago as 1952. He said that *everyone* is entitled to the rights guaranteed by the First Amendment:

> I cannot ... find in our constitutional scheme the power of a state to place its employees in the category of second-class citizens by denying them freedom of thought and expression. The Constitution guarantees freedom of thought and expression to everyone in our society. All are entitled to it; and none needs it more than the teacher. [35]

In this case, Justice Douglas was discussing a law which permitted a hearing to be held to determine whether or not a teacher had ever joined a subversive organization. The teacher could not be present at this hearing, and could only show she was innocent after charges were brought against her. Douglas felt that this procedure was unconstitutional, and said that:

> The very threat of [the procedure used] ... is certain to raise havoc with academic freedom.... Fearing condemnation ..., [the teacher] will tend to shrink from any association that stirs controversy. In that manner freedom of expression will be stifled.
> . . . .
> What happens under this law is typical of what happens in a police state. Teachers are under constant surveillance; their pasts are combed for signs of disloyalty; their utterances are watched for clues to dangerous thoughts. A pall is cast over the classrooms. There can be no real academic freedom in that environment. Where suspicion fills the air and holds scholars in line for fear of their jobs, there can be no exercise of the free intellect.... A deadening dogma takes the place of free inquiry. Instruction tends to become sterile; pursuit of knowledge is discouraged; discussion often leaves off where it should begin.
> ... This system of spying and surveillance with its accompanying reports and trials cannot go hand in hand with academic freedom. It produces standardized thought, not the pursuit of truth. Yet it was pursuit of truth which the First Amendment was designed to protect....
> ... [T]he guilt of the teacher should turn on overt acts. So long as she is a law abiding citizen,

**GUIDE
RULE**

SO LONG AS HER PERFORMANCE WITHIN THE PUBLIC SCHOOL SYSTEM MEETS PROFESSIONAL STANDARDS, HER PRIVATE LIFE, HER POLITICAL PHILOSOPHY, HER SOCIAL CREED SHOULD NOT BE THE CAUSE OF REPRISALS AGAINST HER. [36]

Although, in this 1952 case, Justice Douglas' opinion did not reflect the law, today his opinion reflects the way in which the courts decide such a case. As a result, loyalty oaths which preclude mere advocacy or membership in unpopular or subversive organizations, cannot be made a condition of public employment. Only specific acts which establish that you have the specific intent to actively contribute to the violent overthrow of the government will be sufficient to disqualify you from a teaching position.

KEYS TO DETERMINE IF YOUR ACTS ARE CONSTITUTIONALLY PROTECTED

In the absence of a violation of your constitutional rights, broad discretion is allowed the school board in deciding whether or not to renew your contract (at least if you do not have tenure). Where your rights have been violated, however, courts will not only reinstate you with back pay, but in many instances will give you money for your pain and suffering as well. It is true that the school board will almost always claim that its decision not to renew a teacher's contract was based on reasons having nothing to do with the teacher's constitutional rights. However, the courts are not blind, and if the real reason for the dismissal was, for example, that the teacher had publicly criticized the school board within his rights, the courts will recognize this and will reinstate the teacher.

The standards and tests applied in judging the acceptability of the many varied forms of expression is extensive and often bewildering; but the standards set forth in the *Pickering* case will most often be applied in judging your speech. The four main standards are:

1. Disruption of superior-subordinate relationships;
2. Breach of loyalty or confidentiality;
3. General disruption of the public service;
4. Indication of unfitness from content of the statement.

Aside from these limitations, your speech is protected. You have a right to speak out on public issues or even to criticize the school system or the school board.

What you say in the classroom is also protected speech. Some subjects lend themselves to philosophizing more than do others. The courts will no doubt allow you great latitude, but some situations may require some sort of reasonable relationship between the subject being taught, and the statement made. As a general rule, however, it would seem that no prohibitions or restrictions may be placed on your freedom of speech within the classroom unless it can be shown that your statements *materially and substantially interfere* with the requirements of appropriate discipline in the operation of the school. If there is no such interference, what you say in the classroom may not form the basis for your dismissal.

The rule is not certain, but it would seem that if your appearance is an expression of your personality, heritage, race or culture, it is protected by the First Amendment. Where your appearance does not interfere with discipline in the school, it should not make you susceptible to discharge. Generally, you can wear a neat, clean beard or mustache. The school can reasonably require men to wear neckties; but in certain instances it is possible that your mode of dress might be an expression of your heritage, culture or racial pride, and perhaps considered a protected right.

Your conduct away from school is your own business. If, however, it *clearly* indicates that you are unfit to teach, or your acts render you incapable of properly fulfilling your teaching duties, the school board may rightfully dismiss you.

Teachers have the right to participate in non-partisan political activity without losing their jobs. The courts have not clearly settled the issue when partisan political activity is concerned, but the trend is toward allowing public employees to participate in such campaigns. You may engage in civil rights activities without fearing retaliatory dismissal. You may associate with any people or organizations, even if they are subversive in nature. However, if it can be shown that you have the knowledge and intent to further the unlawful aims of the organization, you may properly be dismissed.

You have many constitutional rights, but remember that your students should be granted one extremely important right: a right to the best possible education you can provide. You have a right to speak, but it is not always wise to do so. You have a right to discuss controversial issues in your classroom, but you should be careful not to let any individual students be unduly hurt. Your personal appearance may be a protected right, but it should not be overly distracting. Knowing the extent of your constitutional rights, you can use them to help improve the educational system and provide your students with an even better education.

FOOTNOTES

1 State v. Turner, 19 So.2d 832 (Fla. 1944).
2 Joyce v. Board of Education, 60 N.E.2d 431 (Ill. 1945), cert. denied, 327 U.S. 786 (1946).
3 391 U.S. 563, 574 (1968).
4 Id. at 572.
5 Puentes v. Board of Education, 250 N.E. 2d 232 (N.Y. 1969).
6 Los Angeles Teacher's Union v. Los Angeles City Board of Education, 455 P.2d 827, 831 (Cal. 1969).
7 Watts v. Seward School Board, 454 P.2d 732 (Alaska 1969), cert. denied, 397 U.S. 921 (1970), rehrg. denied, 397 U.S. 1071 (1970).
8 Alaska Comp. Laws Ann., § 14.20.095 (1966).
9 Keyishian v. Board of Regents, 385 U.S. 589, 603 (1967).
10 Scopes v. State, 289 S.W. 363 (Tenn. 1927).
11 Epperson v. Arkansas, 393 U.S. 97 (1968).
12 Parker v. Board of Education, 237 F. Supp. 222 (U.S. Dist. Ct. Md. 1965), aff'd, 348 F.2d 464 (4th Cir. 1965), cert. denied, 382 U.S. 1030 (1968).
13 Weiman v. Updegraff, 344 U.S. 183, 195 (1952) (concurring opinion).
14 Keefe v. Geanakos, 418 F.2d 359, 361-362 (1st Cir. Mass. 1969).
15 Pred v. Board of Public Instruction of Dade County, 415 F.2d 851 (5th Cir. Fla. 1969).
16 Goldwasser v. Brown, 417 F.2d 1169, 1177 (Dist. Col. Cir. 1969), cert. denied, 397 U.S. 922 (1970).
17 Tinker v. Des Moines School Dist., 393 U.S. 503 (1969).
18 Burnside v. Byars, 363 F.2d 744 (5th Cir. Miss. 1966).
19 Tinker v. Des Moines School Dist., 393 U.S. 503, 508-509 (1969).
20 Finot v. Pasadena City Board of Education, 250 Cal. App. 2d 189, 58 Cal. Rptr. 520, 527 (1967).
21 Id. at 529.
22 Lucia v. Duggan, 303 F. Supp. 112, 118 (U.S. Dist. Ct. Mass. 1969).
23 Braxton v. Board of Public Instruction, 303 F. Supp. 958, 959 (U.S. Dist. Ct. Fla. 1969).
24 U.S. District Court Judge Noel P. Fox. Capital Journal, (Salem, Oregon), Jan. 13, 1971, at 24, col. 2. Judge Fox granted a student's motion for temporary relief. These were off the record remarks.
25 Horosko v. School District of Mount Pleasant, 6 A.2d 866 (Pa. 1939), cert. denied, 308 U.S. 553 (1939).
26 Jarvella v. Willoughby-Eastlake City School District, 233 N.E. 2d 143, 146 (Ohio 1967).
27 Hale v. Board of Education, 234 N.E.2d 583 (Ohio 1968).
28 Morrison v. State Board of Education, 461 P.2d 375, 386 (Cal. 1969).
29 Id. at 386-387.
30 Report of the Sub-committee in Personal Problems of the Assembly Interim Committee of Education, Appendix to the *Journal of the Assembly,* vol. 2, p.25 (Cal. 1965).
31 Watts v. Seward School Board, 454 P.2d 732 (Alaska 1969), cert. denied, 397 U.S. 921 (1970), rehrg. denied, 397 U.S. 1071 (1970).
32 Rackley v. School District No. 5, 258 F. Supp. 679, 684 (U.S. Dist. Ct. S.C. 1966).
33 Keyishian v. Board of Regents, 385 U.S. 589 (1967).
34 Elfbrandt v. Russel, 384 U.S. 11, 17 (1965).
35 Adler v. Board of Education, 342 U.S. 485, 508 (1952) (dissenting opinion).
36 Id. at 509-511.

FIVE

Teaching Under a Contract
with the Board

Signing a contract is easy. Realizing what the extent of your rights and responsibilities are, under that contract, can pose some challenging questions. Every year, contract questions will come up between you and the board. You don't generally worry much about the implied terms of the contract. Instead, you are interested in the provisions as to salaries, the length of the school year, and whether or not the contract is automatically renewable. These are important provisions, but they are among the least significant when it comes to actually working under your agreement.

After you sign a contract, you will become aware of the following facts:

1. Not being properly certified will prevent you from being paid.
2. You must legally accept the contract in the proper manner.
3. When you accept the terms written in the contract, you also accept the responsibility of working under the reasonable rules and regulations of your local board.
4. You have some duties and responsibilities in teaching other than conveying knowledge to your students.
5. You do not have the duty or responsibility of performing menial services, or services unrelated to your educational preparation.
6. Also, there are only special circumstances in which the board can dismiss you from your teaching duties. If you are improperly dismissed, the board is breaking its contract, and will be liable.

A contract is a simple piece of paper with terms printed on its face. It is offered and then accepted by the one to whom the offer is made. After that, it is something under which you work. It signifies mutual agreement, and you and the board must abide by its terms. Your contract must have basic elements, or else it is invalid The contract might tell you whether or not you can be transferred, whether you may have a leave of absence, or whether or not you are expected to wait until after the budget is approved before your contract becomes binding upon the local board.

The contract does not generally express all of your duties, your responsibilities, or the reasons the board might have for dismissing you from your position. No one can write a contract that covers every conceivable problem. Nevertheless, you are expected to know many things without having them written down. That may seem difficult, but it is possible. The courts have outlined your rights and responsibilities under a teaching contract, and all that is necessary is an understanding of how these court opinions affect you and your job of teaching under a contract with the board.

OBTAINING YOUR LICENSE TO TEACH

Before you begin teaching, you must be licensed. This license is usually a certificate to teach at a certain grade level or to hold a special educational position. If you do not have a certificate issued by your state, then school funds cannot generally be spent to pay you for your services. If this were not true, anyone could be employed to teach, and this could easily result in a lower standard of education for students. Therefore, before you begin teaching under a contract, make sure you have an up-to-date certificate.

All states have laws which govern teacher certification. The certificate is a license and not a contract. In order to get this certificate, you must meet the requirements set up by your state. To meet these requirements, you must first prove that you have completed the necessary courses in college. Secondly, you must generally show that you are physically capable of holding down a teaching position. And thirdly, you must show that you have good moral character. Once you meet these requirements, your certificate cannot be denied or revoked unless at a later time you lack the necessary qualifications. This means that your State Board of Education must renew your certificate so long as the requirements are met and no charges of incompetency have been filed against you.

Each state prescribes its own qualifications for certification. It is your responsibility to procure a teaching certificate, and "... in a proceeding to revoke or deny a teaching credential, the primary inquiry concerns [your] fitness to teach and the protection of the pupils who will be influenced...."[1] Generally the State Board of Education is the agency that gives the license. This brings up the question of who and what determines your fitness to teach. The answer is that, so long as your board of education is not acting arbitrarily, it will generally be the agency which decides your fitness to carry a license.

The difficulties in determining fitness were discussed by a New York court which said:

> Exact definition of the qualities which are essential or desirable may be impossible; exact formula or standard by which such qualities may be measured has never been achieved; mechanical application of any standard is certainly not practicable. Much must be left to the judgment of the examiners. The test cannot be wholly objective and to the extent that it is subjective the result may depend as much upon the fitness of the examiners as upon the fitness of the candidate. That is a risk inherent in all systems of examination. . . .
>
> . . . Appeal may be addressed to the courts only where it is made to appear that examiners acted arbitrarily and without application of "measures or standards which are sufficiently objective to be capable of being challenged and reviewed, when necessary, by other examiners of equal ability and experience." [2]

The court here has suggested that objective measures and standards should be defined in order to have a criteria on which fitness is determined. Not all states have these measures and standards spelled out, and if that is the case, a basic ambiguity exists which should be made more definite and certain. In Oregon, for example, there are no such measures or standards. Commission of a felony may be grounds for denial of a certificate. On the other hand, having been a minor in possession of liquor, or having been convicted of drunk driving is not necessarily a basis for denial of a certificate. In addition, there may or may not have been a repetitive pattern to the applicant's actions. All these things need to be taken into consideration. Therefore, there should be clear guidelines as to what constitutes fitness to teach. Your State Board of Education has the right to make up these guidelines, and acts which show a lack of qualifications can be such things as:

1. Being physically or mentally disabled.
2. Having had a certificate previously revoked.
3. Conviction of a felony or a crime involving moral turpitude.
4. Committing fraud in obtaining the certificate.

Generally, the act which shows lack of proper qualifications must adversely affect the teacher-student relationship. If the act is such that it does not affect this relationship, and you are denied a license, there are appeal procedures that you may take in order to procure your certificate.

As previously indicated, showing of good moral character is generally a prerequisite to becoming certified. You must show that you are morally fit to teach. In one case, an applicant for a certificate had been convicted of a burglary many years prior to his application. The man paid for his crime, later went to college, and wanted to become a teacher. The man presented many letters to show that he had a good reputation within his community. The State Board denied the certificate, and the court said that the board acted properly. The court also said that, "In resolving the question of moral character there must be kept in mind the distinction between character and reputation. 'Character is what a man or woman is morally, while reputation is what he or she is reputed to be.'"[3]

The board, in denying certification, must have substantial evidence that the teacher is not morally fit. As one court said:

> Undoubtedly, the character of a potential teacher of school children of immature years is a proper concern of those charged with the responsibility of educating the young and it is likewise a proper concern of the courts in determining whether or not school officials properly perform this function.[4]

This means that it is within the discretionary power of the State Board to determine the quality of the evidence against the teacher However:

GUIDE RULE BOARDS OF EDUCATION ARE AMONG THE *LEAST* POWERFUL OF GOVERNMENTAL AGENCIES AND THE COURTS WILL NOT PERMIT THEIR DISCRETIONARY POWERS TO PRODUCE ARBITRARY REFUSALS OF TEACHING CERTIFICATES. THE MEASURES AND STANDARDS OF THE BOARD MUST BE RELEVANT AND APPROPRIATE TO THE POSITION BEING SOUGHT. WHERE THESE MEASURES AND STANDARDS ARE NOT RELEVANT, THE COURTS WILL LOOK TO SEE IF THE BOARD HAS OVER-STEPPED ITS POWERS.

SIGNING A CONTRACT

Once you have obtained the necessary certificate, you are ready to sign a contract to teach. The wording of teaching contracts may vary, but all contracts must have certain basic elements in order for them to be legally binding on the school board and yourself.

GUIDE RULE TO BE LEGALLY BINDING, A CONTRACT MUST INCLUDE:
1. MUTUAL AGREEMENT TO THE TERMS;
2. CONSIDERATION TO BOTH PARTIES;
3. BOTH PARTIES MUST HAVE THE CAPACITY TO SIGN; and
4. THE CONTRACT MUST BE LAWFUL IN ITS PURPOSE.

Before a court can enforce the parties' rights under a contract, all of the elements are essential. If any of these elements are missing, there is no contract, and no one is legally obligated to follow any of the contract's terms.

Problems can arise in trying to determine whether or not these elements actually exist. In the case of teachers' contracts, more problems than normal seem to occur. This is so because of the basic ambiguity present in most contracts for teachers. As a teacher, you have many implied obligations that are not stated in your contract. Therefore, you should understand your rights and obligations under a contract before you sign.

Mutual Agreement to the Terms.

In the case of your contract to teach, you agree to perform certain services, and the local board agrees to pay you for those services. This agreement comes about through an "offer" which must be clear and definite, and an "acceptance" to that offer. In other words:

> **GUIDE RULE**
>
> AN OFFER SHOULD STATE: (1) THE SERVICES YOU ARE TO RENDER, (2) THE PRICE TO BE PAID FOR THESE SERVICES, (3) THE TIME FOR YOU TO START, AND (4) WHEN THE SERVICES ARE TO BE COMPLETED.

The offer must be made with the "present" intent to enter into a contract. "Future" intent to enter into the contract is considered preliminary negotiation, and cannot be accepted. The offer includes a promise to pay you for your services, if you agree to the terms of the contract. You may accept or reject this offer. If you reject the offer, you may not later accept it without another offer being made, or the original offer being made again. If you do accept the offer, however, there are certain procedures you must follow in order for your acceptance to be valid.

Where the offer is made to you by mail, your acceptance takes effect the moment you drop a letter of acceptance into the mailbox. Once an offer has been accepted, the contract is complete and binding, and the offer cannot generally be revoked. Your acceptance must be clear and definite, and with a present rather than a future intent to be bound by the terms of the contract. Furthermore, you must sign the contract and send it back within the time limit stated by the school board. If no time limit is stipulated, you must accept the offer within a "reasonable" time. If you accept the offer too late, your acceptance is considered a counter offer, which in turn must be accepted by the school board before the contract will be binding.

Capacity to Sign.

If a contract is entered into and one of the parties to the contract lacks the legal capacity to sign, the contract is at least voidable if not totally void. In most states, only the school board is qualified to enter into a contract with a teacher. This means that your contract cannot be signed by just one board member, or by the superintendent. The contract must have been agreed to at a regular or special meeting of the board. Generally, the contract is signed while the board is in session. However, your contract may be signed outside the board meeting, so long as the majority of the board members have previously agreed to the terms of the contract. If you receive a contract that has not gone through the proper procedures with the board, the contract is void.

In addition to the necessity of the board having legal capacity to sign, you must also be legally capable. Therefore:

GUIDE RULE

IF YOU ARE WITHOUT A PROPER TEACHING CERTIFICATE, YOU ARE NOT A COMPETENT PARTY TO A CONTRACT WITH THE BOARD. THIS MEANS THAT AN AGREEMENT BETWEEN YOU AND THE BOARD HAS NO LEGAL EFFECT AND YOU CANNOT BE PAID UNDER THE CONTRACT.

Your certificate, then, is an extremely important piece of paper to have. Some states say that you may sign a contract before you have the proper certificate, but that you must obtain the certificate before you begin teaching. If you teach without the proper certificate, and later obtain one, you can only be paid for those days after you have been certified.

On the other hand, if you are teaching in a state which says you must be certified before signing a contract, you must do so if you do not want the contract declared void. The laws differ under state statutes, and your State Board of Education can provide you with this information. It should be remembered that for each year there is generally a new contract signed. Therefore, you must renew your certificate when necessary. Even though you may automatically be qualified to obtain a certificate, you must secure that certificate before you commence your teaching duties.

A Contract

You may not dictate to the local school board the wording of your contract. You may discuss the contract with the board, but they do not have to make the changes you feel are necessary.

A typical teaching contract is shown in Exhibit 2.

This contract shall be executed in duplicate, the original to be filed with the school district clerk, the duplicate to be retained by the teacher.

To be valid this contract must be authorized at a regular school board meeting and signed by the chairman of the board, the school district clerk and the teacher. In districts with census of less than 1,000 children the teacher shall send the contract, together with the teacher's certificate and health certificate, to the appropriate intermediate education district for registration.

Teacher's Contract

THIS AGREEMENT made this ———— day of ———————————, 19———, by and between School District No. ——— of ——————— County, hereinafter referred to as the district and ———————————, hereinafter referred to as the teacher.

WITNESSETH:

1. The district agrees to employ the teacher for a period of ———— year(s), commencing on the first day of July, 19———, and ending on the 30th day of June, 19———, and to pay the teacher therefor an annual salary of $————————, together with any salary increases and other increments applicable pursuant to salary schedules or compensation programs established by the district.

2. In consideration of the compensation paid hereunder, the teacher agrees to teach ———————— grades
(Elementary or Secondary)

in the schools of the district during the period of the regular school year as established by the district; said school year shall commence on or about the ———— day of ——————— of the calendar year and consist of ———— school days
(Sept., Aug., etc.)

thereafter. School days shall be the consecutive calendar days following commencement of the school year, except Saturdays and Sundays, Christmas and Spring vacation periods as established by the district, and school closures occasioned by fire, flood, epidemic or similar occurrences which, in the judgment of the district, necessitates suspension of school operations.

3. The teacher agrees to well and duly perform all duties of the teaching assignments made by the district and will have and maintain the legal qualifications required to teach the aforesaid grades during all times that performance is required hereunder. "Teaching assignments" as used in this agreement shall include such pupil supervisory assignments as may be required by the district. In addition to the duties to be performed during the school year, the teacher agrees to attend such district orientation programs, in-service training programs or other special programs as required by the district, not to exceed a total of ———————— days preceding or subsequent to the school year.

4. The teacher's annual compensation hereunder shall be paid in ———————— equal monthly installments,
(nine, twelve, etc.)

payable on the last day of each month during which services have been rendered; however, nothing herein shall be construed to prevent the teacher and the district from agreeing in writing to a different payment schedule.

5. Additional terms of the contract are as follows:

6. It is understood and agreed between the parties that the validity and legal effect of this agreement is subject to the applicable laws of the State of ———— the duly adopted rules of the State Board of Education and of the district; by this reference said laws and rules are made a part of this agreement the same as if fully set forth herein.

IN WITNESS WHEREOF School District No. ———— has caused this instrument to be executed in its name by its officers as authorized by resolution of a legally conducted meeting of the district school board held the ———————— day of ————————, 19———;

I agree to the foregoing: Board of Directors of District No. ————————

————————————————————   By ————————————————————
                Teacher   Chairman

————————————————————   By ————————————————————
                Address   Clerk

If this contract is not signed by the teacher and returned to the clerk within ———— days, the board reserves the right to declare said contract void and of no effect.

SP*39156-581   BOARD OF EDUCATION Form 345

EXHIBIT 2

This contract is divided into six paragraphs. The first paragraph includes the basic elements of a contract. The second paragraph begins to outline some of the teaching duties.

Paragraph three is the most difficult to interpret. You should try to have "all duties" and "teaching assignments" specifically listed in your contract. Your extra responsibilities should be in writing, and you should know them before you sign. Of course, not all duties can be stated in a contract.

> . . .[S]uch duties as cafeteria assignments, variety shows, club sponsors and duties at commencements . . . [are valid]. All of these duties are supervisory in nature and a minute detailing of them is quite unnecessary . . . .[5]

Nevertheless, not all teaching duties can be taken for granted, and there are limits to your obligations under a contract. Substantial extra responsibilities should be clearly set forth. If you know what your duties are when you sign the contract, and if the board knows what areas the contract covers, fewer disagreements will occur between you and the board.

Paragraphs four and six are self-explanatory. Paragraph five could be used to clear up some of the ambiguities discussed in paragraph three. If additional terms are added to paragraph five, the terms must be clearly defined, so that both you and the board are absolutely certain of their intent.

Granted, some of these contract problems are difficult to understand. What should be remembered is:

**GUIDE
RULE**
BEFORE YOU ENTER INTO A CONTRACT, BE CERTAIN OF YOUR LEGAL CAPACITY TO SIGN. THEN, WHEN YOU SIGN THE CONTRACT, BE CERTAIN YOUR EXTRA RESPONSIBILITIES AND THE TERMS OF THE CONTRACT ARE CLEARLY SET FORTH IN WRITING.

WORKING UNDER A CONTRACT
WITH THE LOCAL SCHOOL BOARD

Once you have your certificate, and have signed your contract, you are legally able to begin teaching. While carrying out your duties, you must work under rules and regulations set up by your administration and school board. Your school board has the authority to impose reasonable rules and regulations governing your employment. However, these rules and regulations cannot conflict with state laws, or infringe on your basic constitutional rights. In addition, the rules and regulations must not be arbitrary or unreasonable.

Determining what is arbitrary or unreasonable is often rather difficult, but there are basic generalizations which can be made. The rules and regulations of your board are considered part of your contract with the school district. As a teacher you are expected to be familiar with the rules.

To be bound by a rule, it is not necessary for the rule to be made prior to your signing the contract. " '*All* rules and regulations' must . . . include those adopted after as well as before the execution of the teacher's contract."[6] This means that you should keep abreast of the rules adopted by your board after you have signed your contract.

The school board is responsible for assuring quality education for the students within its district. This means that: ". . . school authorities have the right and the duty to screen the officials, teachers and employees as to their fitness to maintain the integrity of the schools . . . ." [7]

In order for the local school board to fulfill its functions, it is given certain discretionary powers. Your local board has the power to establish qualifications beyond those required by the state. Physical examinations and professional growth requirements are common additions to state rules and regulations. Nevertheless, the local board must follow the law; and again, ". . . any by-law of a board outlining teachers' duties must stand the test of reasonableness."[8]

You should remember that:

GUIDE
RULE
     A SCHOOL DISTRICT HAS THE POWER TO DISCHARGE CERTIFICATED PROFESSIONAL PERSONNEL FOR CONTINUED VIOLATION OF ANY LAWFUL RULES OR REGULATIONS OF THE BOARD . . . .[9]

What are lawful rules or regulations that stand the test of reasonableness?

GUIDE
RULE
     RULES AND REGULATIONS WILL BE CONSIDERED VALID WHERE THERE IS A *SUBSTANTIAL* AND *MATERIAL* SCHOOL INTEREST IN HAVING SUCH A RULE. HOWEVER, THE RULE OR REGULATION *CANNOT* INTERFERE WITH YOUR CONSTITUTIONAL RIGHTS OR RIGHTS PROTECTED BY YOUR CONTRACT.

An example of an unreasonable rule or regulation is a case in which the city passed an ordinance requiring all public employees, including teachers, to be or to become residents of the city in which they worked. The court held that a teacher has a fundamental right to live and travel where he chooses. This right could not be restricted unless there was an important public interest, and in the case of teachers (unlike firemen), such an interest does not generally exist.[10]

In addition to the rules and regulations of the board which are a part of your contract, you have basic duties or implied obligations to fulfill as a teacher. You may be expected to:

1. Supervise a study hall or the cafeteria
2. Supervise student meetings and clubs.
3. Direct plays if you are an English teacher.
4. Coach intramural sports if you teach physical education.
5. Supervise educational trips which are properly a part of the school curriculum.
6. Accompany the school band if you teach music.

As a general rule, the duties must relate to the subject you teach, or must be collateral to your classroom activities. For instance, an industrial arts teacher may be required to conduct a cement pouring demonstration, or a physical education teacher may be required to coach basketball. Any teacher might be required to handle money, file lesson plans, keep student records, or attend evening open house for parents at the school. However, you cannot be required to supervise an activity that is outside of the school's services. An example of such an activity might be a bowling club of the students which is not a club under the auspices of the school.

These duties are a part of teaching, and the school board is not required to pay you an additional amount of money for carrying out these services. In essence, however, most teacher bargaining contracts provide that teachers performing certain "extra duties" must be paid extra compensation. Where the assignment is not within the scope of your duty, you do not have to perform. If you teach math, you do not have to be a coach. However, if you would like to coach, there is nothing to prevent the board from paying you for such a service.

The duties assigned must not be discriminatory, punitive or menial. You do not have to perform janitorial services, police services or busing tasks. The following guide rule should serve as a key to determine whether or not a duty assigned is valid.

GUIDE RULE   SUPERVISING THE STUDENTS AND BEING PRESENT TO PROTECT THEIR WELFARE AT SCHOOL ATHLETIC AND SOCIAL ACTIVITIES, CONDUCTED UNDER THE NAME AND AUSPICES OF THE SCHOOL, IS WITHIN THE SCOPE OF THE CONTRACT AND SUCH ASSIGNMENTS ARE PROPER SO LONG AS THEY ARE DISTRIBUTED IMPARTIALLY, THEY ARE REASONABLE IN NUMBER AND HOURS OF DUTY AND EACH TEACHER HAS HIS SHARE OF SUCH DUTY.[11]

Closely allied to the duties a board may place on the teacher in the classroom is the power of the board to transfer a teacher to another school or grade level. This power is not absolute, but it should be recognized. If you sign a contract to teach, and you prefer a special school, that school should be listed in the contract. In addition to the school being named in the contract, there should be a provision that you are not subject to transfer while the contract is in force. In the absence of such a provision:

GUIDE RULE
YOU MAY BE ASSIGNED OR TRANSFERRED TO A DIF-FERENT GRADE LEVEL OR SCHOOL SO LONG AS YOU ARE QUALIFIED TO HOLD THAT POSITION AND THE BOARD HAS NOT ACTED ARBITRARILY OR IN BAD FAITH. THE TRANS-FER MUST BE REASONABLE AND SHOULD EITHER BE DUE TO AN EMERGENCY OR SERVE IN THE SUBSTANTIAL BEST INTERESTS OF THE SCHOOL.

If your prior position has been abolished, you must be transferred to an equal position if such a position is available. If you are not transferred to such a position when you have that right, you may hold the board liable for any losses you might incur as a direct result of their breaking their contract obligations.

STEPS IN RENEWING A CONTRACT

After you have worked for six or seven months in a district, you might begin thinking about working at the same school for another year. There are certain laws your board and you must follow in renewing a contract. There are additional procedures in offering and accepting a contract, and there are budget considerations you should be aware of.

In most districts not governed by Teacher Tenure Laws (discussed in Chapter Six), the general law is that:

1. Your school board must give you notice before a certain date as to renewal or non-renewal of your contract.
2. If your board fails to give proper notice, your contract is considered renewed at a salary not less than what you are presently receiving.
3. Where you have not received proper notice, your contract will not be automatically renewed unless you give proper notice of your acceptance before a certain date.
4. Where you have given proper notice, and the board has not, you have a valid contract which the board must issue.

Notice from Your Board.

Most states require the board to give proper notice of their intention not to renew a contract. The notice must comply with state laws. The wording of the notice must be explicit in order to clearly convey its meaning. If the notice is ambiguous or obscure, it is insufficient and can be disregarded. In other words, the notice must sufficiently inform you of the board's intent not to renew your contract.

In addition to the requirement that the notice be clearly stated, there is ordinarily a minimum time period within which the notice must be received. When the notice is not received within the proper time limit, the notice is generally void, and you are entitled to another contract. Dates can play an important part in notice requirements. Where the law says that you must receive the notice within a certain time, you must receive it within that time. If the law states that you must receive such notice on or before the 15th of March, then that is the final date. If the board should send notice later than that date, or send it on March 15th, and you receive it on March 16th, then you are still entitled to a contract.

As you can see, there is a form and manner in which the notice must be given. If the law says written notice, oral notice is not valid. If the law says the letter must be sent by registered or certified mail to your last known address, placing the letter into your mailbox in the faculty room is not sufficient. The board must follow proper procedures in conveying its intent, and if it does not follow these procedures, you are entitled to a contract.

You must also follow proper procedures in accepting a renewed contract. Generally, you will be required to sign the contract by a certain date, and return the contract in a specified manner. If you do not follow this procedure, your contract is considered abandoned and void.

<table>
<tr><td></td><td>INHERENT IN THE BOARD'S RIGHT TO CONTRACT WITH ITS TEACHERS [IS] THE RIGHT TO ESTABLISH A REASONABLE TIME WITHIN WHICH AN OFFER TO A CONTRACT CAN BE</td></tr>
<tr><td>**GUIDE**
RULE</td><td>ACCEPTED . . . .

IF, AFTER HAVING BEEN TIMELY OFFERED THE CONTRACT . . . A TEACHER FAILS TO ACCEPT OR REJECT IT WITHIN THE REASONABLE TIME ALLOWED, THE BOARD MUST BE RELEASED FROM ITS OBLIGATION.[12]</td></tr>
</table>

Notice requirements are extremely beneficial laws. They help the school board plan ahead. By knowing which teachers intend to resign, the board has plenty of time to interview and hire replacements. On the other hand, you are given notice whether or not your contract is to be renewed, and if it is not, you have time to interview in other districts.

Problems have arisen where a teacher has signed a contract prior to a budget election since, if the budget is defeated, money is not available in order to fulfill the terms of the contract. Because of such lack of money, a question arises whether, in such case, the board is bound by its prior contract obligations, or whether the teacher is bound if he then decides to seek employment elsewhere. School boards propose what they feel is a necessary budget. They may sign contracts in reliance on their budget proposals. Nevertheless, the school's budget is generally subject to voter approval, and if approval is not given, the contract with the teacher is voidable. The board may "re-offer" a new contract, with different terms; and you are not obligated to accept the new offer, but you should give notice of your intent.

Your contract cannot be modified without your consent. The board may reduce your projected salary in the event a budget proposal is defeated, but it cannot force you to accept the reduction. In such case, you may consider your contract void, and you will have no obligation to perform.

This should not prevent you from contracting with a board before a budget election. You must simply wait for voter approval to see whether your contract, as written, will be the final agreement, or whether you must be offered a new contract due to budgetary reductions. If you do not accept the new offer, you are not under obligation under the prior contract, and you cannot suffer penalties for failure to accept a contract with different terms.

DISMISSALS AND BREACH OF CONTRACT

So far we have discussed the signing of a contract and performing of obligations under the written document. What happens, though, when you or the board breaks or breaches a promise under the contract? When can you resign, have a leave of absence, or be suspended or dismissed from your position? Not all dismissals are proper, and an improper dismissal can result in a monetary award to the injured teacher. The courts can overrule improper school board decisions; and where the board has overstepped its discretionary powers, a teacher may be reinstated.

Resignations and Abandonment.

Most all states have laws governing the resignation of teachers. There are times when you can resign without penalty. On the other hand, there are times when an improper resignation could result in a suspension or revocation of your teaching certificate. Generally, you cannot resign your teaching position while school is in session, or from 60 to 90 days before school is to begin. If you do resign without the board's permission, your conduct might be deemed "unprofessional," and your teaching certificate may be suspended or even revoked in some states.

Your local school board cannot suspend your certificate. In order to do so, it must notify the State Board of Education which, in turn, may or may not make the suspension. Your certificate is not *automatically* suspended. It will partially depend on whether the local board decides to give the state notice. If your certificate is suspended, you may appeal the decision through proper channels.

This does not mean that you can never resign without penalty. Incapacity to perform is a valid reason for leaving your position. Furthermore, you may be released from your contract if the local board gives its permission. Where permission has been given, the board cannot later complain to the State Board of Education.

If you have signed a contract for an upcoming year, and later decide not to perform, you may be released from your obligation if you give notice of your intent prior to the 60 or 90 days (depending upon your particular state) before school is to begin. This period of time gives the local board an opportunity to find a replacement without much difficulty, and therefore, you should not be penalized.

Resigning "during" the school year can present some complications. If your resignation is due to necessity, there will generally be no problems. Of course, you must give notice and follow the proper procedures. If your local board has valid reasons for wanting you to resign, they must also follow proper procedures. This fact was illustrated in a California case in which the teacher involved claimed that his resignation was invalid because of acts on the part of his superintendent. The teacher involved claimed that he lacked the capacity to resign, due to severe mental and emotional strain as a result of his having been arrested, questioned, booked on a criminal charge, and released without having slept for 40 hours. Immediately after this release, his superintendent came to his apartment and asked for a resignation. The teacher had had no time to consult with an attorney, and the superintendent threatened that, unless the resignation was forthcoming, he would publicize the arrest at a board meeting, and cause the teacher to suffer embarrassment and humiliation. The court found that the superintendent used undue influence, and the court ordered that the teacher be reinstated. The court said undue influence is:

> ... persuasion which tends to be coercive in nature, persuasion which overcomes the will without convincing the judgment....The hallmark of such persuasion is high pressure, a pressure which works on mental, moral, or emotional weakness to such an extent that it approaches the boundaries of coercion. In this sense, undue influence has been called over-persuasion.... By statutory definition undue influence includes "taking an unfair advantage of another's weakness of mind; or ... taking a grossly oppressive and unfair advantage of another's necessities or distress."[13]

This means that you cannot be "coerced" into signing a resignation where persuasion to sign is not sufficient. In addition to the necessity of having legal capacity to "sign" a contract, you must have legal capacity to "resign" the same. The court in this case went on to say that "a party may be led but not driven, and his acts must be the offspring of his own volition, and not the record of someone else's."

Once you have resigned, it may be difficult to get reinstated after a change of heart. You may retract a resignation if you do so before the resignation has been accepted, or before the board has done some act in reliance on your stated intent. However, even accepted resignations have been held ineffective under certain circumstances.

There may be days in teaching where the frustrations have mounted, and you feel that your best alternative is to walk out the door. Such action is not recommended, but it has occurred. In one such case, a teacher had a misunderstanding with the head of her department which resulted in a heated argument with her principal, the superintendent, and the head of her school board. The teacher attempted to resolve the argument, but ended up crying, angry, dazed, shocked and discouraged. After school that day, she resigned. That night, a special meeting was held by the board for a different reason, but at the meeting, her resignation was accepted. She did not know about the meeting, and she attempted to rescind her resignation a day later. She argued in court that her resignation was invalid, as it was the product of duress. Even though the court found that there was no actual duress, they gave her relief due to the extraordinary circumstances and events. The court pointed out that she could have rescinded her resignation if there had not been a special meeting of the board. Furthermore, she attempted to rescind her resignation promptly, and the board had not yet hired someone to take her place. Although the teacher was not awarded her back salary, she was reinstated.[14]

GUIDE
RULE
IF YOU RESIGN AND LATER CHANGE YOUR MIND, YOU MUST ACT PROMPTLY TO RESCIND YOUR RESIGNATION. YOU MAY RETRACT A RESIGNATION WHERE IT HAS NOT BEEN ACCEPTED OR WHERE THE BOARD HAS NOT DONE A SUBSTANTIAL ACT IN RELIANCE OF YOUR STATED INTENT.

Closely allied to improper resignations are improper strikes on the part of the teacher. Private employees have the right to strike, but in nearly all states, public employees do not have that right. In a Minneapolis school teachers' strike in 1970, the court said that, as a teacher, you lack the right to strike, "... particularly when legislative enactments prohibit strikes against a public entity as being unlawful."[15] This means that a strike is an unjustified failure to perform your promise to teach, and you are therefore breaking your contract obligations by doing so.

**GUIDE
RULE**

WHEN YOU UNLAWFULLY STRIKE OR LEAVE YOUR TEACH-ING POSITION, YOU HAVE ABANDONED YOUR CONTRACT AND YOUR EMPLOYMENT IS TERMINATED. YOU NO LONGER HOLD YOUR TEACHING POSITION AND YOU CAN-NOT BE PAID UNDER YOUR CONTRACT WITHOUT BEING REAPPOINTED.

A school board will generally reappoint a large striking body of teachers. The school board is not necessarily bound to consider the strike as a total breach of contract, but only a partial one. In that event, the board may treat the contract as continuing. The board may not pay the striking teacher nor charge the teacher a fee for reinstatement. Strikes are more fully discussed in Chapter Seven.

Leaves of Absence:

School boards may establish almost any type of leave of absence. Types of leave are usually in the stated policies of the board. In addition to the board's leave of absence policies, the state usually makes certain leaves of absence mandatory. Common among mandatory leaves of absence are (a) sick leave; (b) military leave; (c) Peace Corps leave; and (d) maternity leave.

A. *Sick leave.* Almost every school district must allow a teacher a certain amount of sick leave with full pay for the days absent. The number of days may vary, and many states allow sick leave to accumulate and to be transferred to other districts within the same state. If sickness is prolonged over many weeks or months, the contract may be considered terminated.

> ... [T]he basic consideration in determining whether an employer may treat a contract of employment as terminated because of the illness or disability of his employee is the effect of the disability upon the performance of the contract.
>
> Thus, where an illness or disability is permanent or covers a considerable portion of the term of the contract, the employer may justifiably treat the contract as terminated in the absence of a contractual provision to the contrary.
>
> However, where the sickness or disability is of brief duration as compared to the term of the contract, it may not ordinarily be treated as terminated, unless by reason of the particular factors surrounding the contract, it is

affected in a substantial sense by the absence of the employee. Factors to be considered are the nature and duration of the disability, the nature of the services to be rendered, the term of the contract, the necessities of the employer, and the availability of a replacement.[16]

B. *Military leave.* If a teacher has been employed by a school district a stated number of months (this varies, and is usually six months) he must be granted a leave of absence to perform his duties for the National Guard or military reserve training. There is a time limit on the number of days he may be on active duty (usually 15 days), and when he returns, he is entitled to the same benefits as when he left. In addition, a teacher cannot be removed from his position for serving in regular military duty. His pay may be suspended during his service, but he may not be penalized in any other way.

C. *Peace Corps.* A teacher may join the Peace Corps and be granted a leave of absence for at least two years. During that time, his pay may be suspended, but there should not be any other consequences as a result of his service.

D. *Maternity Leave.* For some reason, many school boards of the past felt that a female teacher should remain unmarried. Many positions were taken, and many reasons were asserted for such a position. Upon one teacher's marriage, a Pennsylvania school board unsuccessfully attempted to dismiss a teacher on the grounds of "immorality." The court held that marriage does not constitute immorality;[17] but what happens when children enter the picture? One school board asserted that a married teacher should be dismissed from her position on the grounds that giving birth to a child constituted an act of "negligence." The court found the board's position absurd, and the teacher was reinstated. [18] However, still another board dismissed a teacher for "incompetency" when her pregnancy prevented her from performing her teaching duties. Although the dismissal was upheld,[19] such a ruling is questionable today. Today, a married teacher who becomes pregnant should not be dismissed, but should be granted a leave of absence whether she has tenure or not.

Maternity leaves for tenured and probationary teachers is a relatively new development, and can present some interesting questions. Case law has not fully covered all situations. However, a few 1971 cases have discussed some of the problems, and a general course of direction can be plotted. In one case, a school board had the policy of granting maternity leaves to tenured teachers, but not to those without tenure status.   To obtain such a leave of absence, the teacher had to submit a written application for maternity leave one month prior to its effective date, and leave four months prior to the expected date of the child's birth. These rules were not at issue, but are questionable. The teacher involved did not have tenure, and was therefore denied the leave of absence. In reversing the board's decision, the court said:

> ...the basis for the policy...which grants maternity leave to tenured teachers and denies it to untenured teachers must be rational and must bear some relevance to the purpose of the tenure act.[20]

The purpose of tenure acts is to protect competent and qualified teachers as to the security of their positions. The rule here was therefore arbitrary and unrelated. The court went on to say that:

> Just as [the school board] grant[s] study leave, bereavement leave, personal illness leave, emergency leave, and military service leave to both tenured and untenured teachers, so, too, must they grant maternity leave to both tenured and untenured teachers.

Assuming future courts will follow this decision (quite possibly they will, but it is not an absolute certainty), the question arises as to when the teacher must stop teaching. Most school districts provide for a mandatory absence at various stages of the pregnancy. It may vary from three, four or five months before the expected date of birth. Such a requirement is now quite questionable. In a 1971 case, a teacher challenged a school board rule that a pregnant teacher must cease her duties four months before the expected birth of the child. The teacher in this case was a probationary teacher, and the court found that there was no medical reason for the board's regulation; and, in fact, pointed out that a person who is pregnant is more likely to miss teaching days in the first four months of pregnancy rather than the last four. The court ruled that:

> ...decisions of when a pregnant teacher should discontinue working are matters best left up to the woman and her doctor.
> . . . .
> The maternity policy of the School Board denies pregnant women... equal protection of the laws because it treats pregnancy differently than other medical disabilities. Because pregnancy, though unique to women, is like other medical conditions, the failure to treat it as such amounts to discrimination which is without rational basis, and therefore is violative of the equal protection clause of the Fourteenth Amendment.[21]

This is an astounding decision, and may force many boards to rewrite their policies on these matters. For example, the Bloomfield and New Medford Boards of Education in New Jersey permit all tenured and non-tenured teachers to work throughout their pregnancy. A teacher may only be relieved if her condition affects her teaching performance, or for "just cause." What constitutes an effect on teaching performance or "just cause" will be a question of fact depending on the circumstances of each case. Furthermore, a teacher who is pregnant may not be removed for medical reasons without a doctor's certificate stating she is unable to perform. If the teacher's doctor and the board's doctor disagree, the doctors pick an impartial third doctor, and his decision is binding. Carrying these requirements a step further, the teacher is also permitted to return to work without a forced "waiting period" after the birth of her child.

Summarizing these last two cases, it seems that forced resignation because of pregnancy is unconstitutional, and a board may not discriminate simply on the basis of sex. The issue is one of fairness to both the teacher and her students. If her condition adversely affects her teaching performance, she should be granted a leave of absence. However, WHEN does her condition do this? Of course, it depends upon the circumstances. The adverse effect must be *actual,* and should be shown as a matter of fact. The decision cannot rest on a value judgment, but should rest on a medical fact, or upon an actual adverse effect (not upon what someone might think or say) upon her teaching performance.

Dismissals.

If you break your contract, you are subject to dismissal. There are many grounds upon which the board may legally make such a decision, and there are many "offenses" justifying dismissal. The most common grounds for dismissal are:

1. Incompetency.
2. Immorality.
3. Insubordination.
4. Physical or mental disability.
5. Unfitness or inadequate performance.
6. Services are no longer needed, due to a decrease in students, courses, positions or schools.
7. Conviction of a felony or a crime involving moral turpitude.
8. Failure to show normal improvement in professional training and growth.
9. Any cause which constitutes grounds for the revocation of your teaching certificate.

1. *Incompetency.* Incompetency is the cause most often cited as grounds for dismissing a teacher.

GUIDE RULE "INCOMPETENCY" IS A RELATIVE TERM WHICH MAY BE EMPLOYED AS MEANING DISQUALIFICATION, INABILITY OR INCAPACITY. IT CAN REFER TO LACK OF LEGAL QUALIFICATIONS OR FITNESS TO DISCHARGE THE REQUIRED DUTY. IT MAY BE EMPLOYED TO SHOW WANT OF PHYSICAL OR INTELLECTUAL OR MORAL FITNESS.[22]

The word "incompetency" seems to involve nearly all of the grounds for dismissal. However, it is not as broad as it may seem. In order for one to be dismissed for incompetency, there must be some objective proof that he is not competent to hold his position as a teacher. Examples of where incompetency has been said to exist are:

A. Where the teacher lacks proper knowledge of the subject.[23]
B. Where the teacher is unable to impart his knowledge to students.[24]
C. Where the teacher is unable to maintain discipline.[25]
D. Where the teacher has physically mistreated students.[26]
E. Where valid rules and regulations have been broken.[27]
F. Where the teacher is unable to get along with school officials due to his own fault or inadequacies.[28]

> Incompetency ordinarily manifests itself in a pattern of behavior, rather than a single incident, and it has been held that the incompetency in the past of a teacher or principal has relevance to the question of the present competency of such person, and that such prior incompetency, at least with respect to the same position, may be used to prove the present incompetency of the teacher or principal so as to justify his dismissal.[29]

Incompetency of a teacher must be reasonably related to his teaching effectiveness, and an isolated instance is not generally valid as a cause for dismissal. Where there is proof of incompetency, and the incidents are related to the teacher's effectiveness in the classroom, a dismissal is valid. However, teachers have been subjected to dismissal proceedings for alleged incompetency where incompetency did not, in fact, exist. A few examples of such, where the court has *not* upheld a dismissal, are:

1. Where the teacher did not maintain harmonious relations with other teachers, but was otherwise a good instructor.[30]
2. Upon complaints from parents where there was no other evidence.[31]
3. Where the teacher got married without telling the board.[32]

2. Immorality. Immorality is another cause frequently cited as grounds for dismissing a teacher. The problem in using immorality as a grounds for dismissal is in determining what immorality actually consists of, and by whose standards it is measured. Some laws say that immorality is manifested when one is convicted of a felony or a crime involving moral turpitude. This is probably true, but it is not restricted to that. There are many acts which may demonstrate a lack of good moral character. For example, failure to disclose a physical defect, or cheating on a certification examination have been held as valid indications of a lack of moral character.

Determining whether a teacher has good moral character is generally the proper function of your State Board of Education which issues you your certificate. However, this power is not absolute, and the local board takes many other things into consideration.

> The word "immoral" is defined generally as that which is hostile to the welfare of the general public and contrary to good morals.
>
> "Immorality" is not necessarily confined to matters sexual in their nature; it may be that which is ... inconsistent with rectitude, purity, or ... contrary to conscience or moral law.... Its synonyms are: corrupt, indecent, depraved, desolute; and its antonyms are: decent, upright, good ... "Immoral" is defined as contrary to good order or public welfare; inimical to the rights or common interests of others .... [33]

If a teacher's conduct could fit into this last definition, there would be a valid ground on which to base his dismissal. Nevertheless, the board must be careful to make certain that the teacher's so-called immorality has a direct relation to his fitness in the classroom, or to his functions within the school.

GUIDE **RULE**	TO BE CONSIDERED IMMORAL, THE CONDUCT MUST BE "... HOSTILE TO THE WELFARE OF THE GENERAL PUBLIC; MORE SPECIFICALLY ... CONDUCT WHICH IS HOSTILE TO THE WELFARE OF THE SCHOOL COMMUNITY.... THE BOARD CAN ONLY BE CONCERNED WITH 'IMMORAL CONDUCT' TO THE EXTENT THAT IT IS, IN SOME WAY, INIMICAL TO THE WELFARE OF THE SCHOOL COMMUNITY." [34]

3. *Insubordination.* In addition to specified contract provisions, you are obligated to comply with the reasonable rules and regulations of your school board. Furthermore, you are expected to cooperate with the administration within your school building. This means that you should refrain from doing acts which interfere with the performance of the administration's duties. In other words, if you disrupt or impede the educational process, there may be grounds for dismissal due to insubordination.

An example of insubordination was a case in which a teacher was charged, in part, with willful neglect of duty. In this instance, the teacher refused to let the principal observe his classes in an effort to help evaluate and improve the teacher's mode and methods of instruction. Later, he refused to let a consultant come into his classroom to assist him in the development of new techniques and procedures, as well as the preparation of materials and demonstrations. The teacher was asked to change his attitude toward visitors, but refused to allow anyone into his classroom for the purpose of observing his teaching performance.

These acts on the part of the teacher were found to be valid grounds for his dismissal.[35] He was expected to cooperate with school officials, and the regulations seem reasonable under the circumstances. Most districts require a teacher to be observed in his classroom a certain number of times during the year. Districts use these observations in order to help evaluate a teacher's effectiveness. Such observation cannot generally be refused. There may be times when you feel that the person observing you is biased, or will not give you a fair appraisal. If such is the case, it seems reasonable that you request that someone else, with the same authority and experience, make the necessary evaluation. You cannot impede the educational process by excluding any and all who might need to come inside your classroom.

4. *Physical or Mental Disability.* Physical or mental disability can be a valid ground for dismissal where the disability will involve long periods of absence from, and ineffectiveness in your teaching duties. Such things as lack of hearing, drug addiction, alcoholism or a serious psychological disability are examples of conditions which could make a teacher ineffective in the classroom. However, these disabilities must *actually* interfere with that effectiveness.

5. *Unfitness or Inadequate Performance.* One of the more ambiguous grounds for dismissal is termed "unfitness" or "inadequate performance." Determining what is unfit or inadequate can sometimes be a difficult process. The courts have discussed it, and the general rule is that unfitness is determined by the impropriety of a teacher's act under the circumstances of each case.

Many times, questions of unfitness or inadequate performance come up in cases where the teacher has discussed a controversial subject, or spoken words which might be considered offensive to others. Swearing in class, or presenting materials containing objectionable words or descriptions is allowable if presented in the proper way. If the profanity is thought-provoking, or for an educational purpose, it will be considered proper. If the material presented is scholarly, thoughtful, thought-provoking or for educational purposes, it is also proper for presentation. It should be remembered that:

> ... [W]hat is to be said or read to students is not to be determined by obscenity standards for adult consumption .... At the same time, the issue must be one of degree. A high school senior is not devoid of all discrimination or resistance. Furthermore, as in all other instances, the offensiveness of language and the particular propriety or impropriety is dependent on the circumstances of the utterance.[36]

You must take into account the age, intelligence and maturity of your students. What is proper material for one class will not necessarily be proper for another.

There are limits to what you may say and discuss in your classroom. You should not discuss subjects of personal interest and opinion which have no relation to the subject you teach. Also, you should be careful in discussing sensitive subjects like race, religion and sex. The manner in which you discuss such subjects may rightfully raise questions as to your fitness to teach. In one case, for example, a teacher was validly discharged, not because he discussed sex, but because of "... the impropriety of his manner of discussing sex before his speech classes and not the factor of the class time consumed in such discussions."[37] There have also been instances where teachers have verbally attacked racial groups. Such lack of objectivity and discretion clearly raises questions regarding fitness to teach.

Classroom conduct is not the sole basis in determining fitness. Outside activities may determine fitness, but only where there is a substantial effect on the teacher's ability to perform in the classroom. Nevertheless, being the center of controversy in a community does not constitute a valid cause for dismissal, and is not an indication of unfitness or inadequacy. There must be a material and substantial interference with the efficiency and discipline in the operation of the school for there to be a valid dismissal under these circumstances. This thought might be carried a step further. Even if you are the center of controversy and there is a substantial interference with the operation of the school, if you are the center of controversy through no fault of your own, you cannot be dismissed for that reason.

Dismissal Procedures.

If dismissal proceedings are taken against you, there are certain statutory procedures that the school board must follow in order for the dismissal to be valid. These procedures are discussed fully in Chapter Six. For now, the thing to keep in mind is that:

GUIDE **RULE**	IF DISMISSAL PROCEEDINGS ARE TAKEN AGAINST YOU *DURING THE TERM OF YOUR CONTRACT,* YOU ARE ENTITLED TO: (1) A STATEMENT OF THE REASONS, (2) A NOTICE OF A HEARING AT WHICH YOU CAN RESPOND TO THE STATED REASONS, AND (3) THE ACTUAL HOLDING OF SUCH A HEARING.

If proper dismissal procedures are not followed, you will be compensated whether the grounds are valid or not. If the proper procedures are followed. but the grounds for your dismissal are unfounded, you will still be entitled to reinstatement

It might be pointed out that:

> In the absence of any statutory or contractual provision to the contrary, the mere fact that a teacher's services are no longer necessary will not justify the dismissal of the teacher without compensation prior to the expiration of his period of employment under a valid contract fixing a definite period of employment.[38]

If you are dismissed or paid less because your services are no longer needed, the school board is breaching your contract. Teachers have been allowed to collect their contract salaries in such cases as:

1. Destruction of the school by fire or tornado.
2. Refusal of parents to send their children to school.
3. Where the board has failed to furnish adequate school facilities.
4. Where the school has been closed due to lack of funds.
5. Abolition of contracted for department prior to commencement of the school term.
6. Reduction of the school term for farm working children.

Damages.

There might be times when you want to be reinstated in your old position after the board has improperly dismissed you. On the other hand, you might seek other damages which do not involve reinstatement. If the board has wrongfully breached your contract, you may collect your lost wages, some of your monetary fringe benefits, your expenses in obtaining similar employment, and your retirement benefits. In other words, you will "receive a sum which, when added to the benefits already received under the contract, will give an economic status identical to that which (you) would have enjoyed had the contract been performed . . .

GUIDE RULE   [YOU ARE] ENTITLED TO DAMAGES EQUIVALENT TO THE AMOUNT OF ACTUAL LOSS SUSTAINED, BE IT LOSS OF BENEFITS OR ADVANTAGES OR EXPENSES WHICH WOULD REASONABLY RESULT FROM A COMPLETE PERFORMANCE ON [YOUR] PART.[39]

During the period in which you are wrongfully dismissed, you are expected to seek other employment. You may collect your expenses, and the amount you earn is deducted from the contract price the board owes. If you do not seek other employment, and it can be shown that other jobs were available to you, what you could have earned will be deducted from the contract amount. However,

**GUIDE
RULE**

YOU ARE NOT REQUIRED TO ACCEPT EMPLOYMENT WHEN IT IS OF A DIFFERENT OR INFERIOR KIND, OR LOCATED A GREAT DISTANCE AWAY. FURTHERMORE, IF THE JOB YOU OBTAIN COULD HAVE BEEN CARRIED ON WHILE YOU WERE UNDER YOUR CONTRACT, THE MONEY YOU EARN WILL NOT BE DEDUCTED FROM WHAT THE BOARD OWES YOU. (Example: Working evenings part-time in unrelated jobs.)

SUMMARY

As you can see, there are a great many things you should know about your contract. The contract covers the basic rights and responsibilities of both you and your board, and it is generally a simple piece of paper with terms that are offered and accepted.

When you accept the terms of the contract, you should be properly licensed to teach by the state. If the license and the contract are both valid, you are expected to perform all of your legal obligations. This means that you must follow the reasonable rules and regulations set up by your local board. You must perform the extra duties that are within the auspices of the school, or collateral to your teaching assignment. However, you do not have to perform duties which are not within the scope of your employment, or those that are arbitrarily placed upon you.

To avoid difficulties in determining which assignments are proper and which are not, you should try to have your duties outlined within the contract before you sign. If this is not possible, the duties should be distributed impartially, and they should be reasonable in number and hours.

If the board does not want to renew your contract for the following year, it must follow proper procedures as set out by your state. On the other hand, if the board does offer you a renewal, you must also follow the proper procedures of acceptance. If the guidelines are followed, you should not experience any difficulties.

Once you have begun working under a contract with the board, you may not be dismissed unless you have done some act which is, in some way, inimical to the welfare of the school. If you are improperly dismissed, the board is violating its contract premises. You will be compensated for any losses which you might incur as a direct result of the board's breach, and you may collect your damages in various ways.

Your contract to teach is one of the most important things protecting your rights and responsibilities in the classroom. The contract is signed by you and the board, and it is an agreement binding both parties. If you and the board understand the contract's purposes and limitations, your respective positions will seldom come into conflict.

FOOTNOTES

1 Alford v. Department of Education, 13 Cal. App.3d 884, 91 Cal Rptr. 843, 846 (Cal. 1971).

2 Sloat v. Board of Examiners of Bd. of Ed. 274 N.Y. 367, 9 N.E.2d 12, 15 (Ct. App., N.Y. 1937).

3 Application of Bay, 378 P.2d 558, 561 (Or. 1963).

4 James v. West Virginia Board of Regents, 322 F. Supp. 217, 228 (D.C., W.Va. 1971).

5 McGrath v. Burkhard, 131 Cal. App. 2d 367, 280 P.2d 864, 868 (Cal. 1955).

6 School City of East Chicago v. Sigler, 36 N.E.2d 760, 763 (Ind. 1941).

7 Adler v. Board of Education, 342 US 485, 96 L ed. 517, 72 S.CT. 380 (1952).

8 Parrish v. Moss, 106 N.Y.S. 2d 577, 584 (Sup. Ct., Sp.T., N.Y. 1951).

9 Heine v. School Dist. No. 271, 481 P.2d 316, 317 (Ida. 1971).

10 Donnelly v. City of Manchester, 274 A.2d 789 (N.H. 1971).

11 McGrath v. Burkhard, 131 Cal. App.2d 367, 280 P.2d 864, 870 (Cal. 1955).

12 Swick v. Seward School Board, 379 P.2d 97, 102 (Alaska 1963).

13 Odorizzi v. Bloomfield School District, 246 Cal. App. 2d 123, 54 Cal Rptr 533, 539 (Cal. 1966).

14 Evaul v. Camden Board of Education, 35 N.J. 244, 172 A.2d 654 (N.J. 1961).

15 Head v. Special School Dist. No. 1, 288 Minn. 496, 182 N.W.2d 887, 894 (Minn. 1970) *rehearing den.* 1971. U.S. App. Pdng.

16 21 ALR2d 1247, 1248 Discharge of Employee—Illness (1952).

17 Appeal of Thomas, 39 Lack. Jur. 41 (Pa. Com. Pleas 1938).

18 In re Leakey, 46 D.&C. 250, 43 Lack.Jur. 227 (Pa. Com. Pleas 1943).

19 West Mahanoy Tp.School District v. Kelly, 156 Pa. Super. 601, 41 A.2d 344 (Pa. 1945).

20 Jinks v. Mays, 332 F.Supp. 254, 257, 259 (D.C., Ga. 1971).

21 Cohen v. Chesterfield County School Board, 326 F.Supp. 1159, 1160, 1161 (D.C., Va. 1971).

22 County Board of Education of Clarke County v. Oliver, 116 So. 2d 566, 567 (Ala. 1959).

23 Board of Education v. Ballou, 21 Cal. App. 2d 52 68 P.2d 389 (Cal. 1937).

24 Briggs v. School City of Mt. Vernon 45 Ind. App. 572, 90 N.E. 105 (Ind. 1909).

25 Robel v. Highline Public Schools, District No. 401, 389 P.2d 1 (Wash. 1965).

26 Berry v. Arnold School District, 137 S.W. 2d 256 (Ark. 1940).

27 Tichenor v. Orleans Parish School Board, 144 So.2d 603 (La. App. 1962).

28 Griggs v. Board of Trustees of Merced Union H.S. District, 61 Cal. Rptr.2d 93, 389 P.2d 722 (Cal. 1964).

29 4 ALR 3d 1090, 1095, Teachers'—Incompetency—Inefficiency, (1965).

30 Compton v. School Directors, 8 Ill. App. 2d 243, 131 N.E.2d. 544 (Ill. 1955) *rehearing den.* 1956.

31 Gulich Tp. School District v. Korman, 31 D & C 197 (Pa. Com. Pleas 1938).

32 McKay v. State, 212 Ind. 338, 7 N.E.2d 954 (Ind. 1937).

33 Words and Phrases, Vol. 20, paraphrased, pp. 226-227. West Publishing Company. St. Paul, Minn. 1959.

34 Jarvella v. Willoughby—Eastlake City School Dist., 41 O. Ops. 2d 423, 233 NE 2d 143, 145(Ohio 1967).

35 Tichenor v. Orleans Parish School Board, 144 So.2d 603 (La. App. 1962).

36 Keefe v. Geanakos, 418 F.2d 359, 362 (1st Cir., Mass. 1969).

37 State v. Board of School Directors of Milwaukee, 111 N.W.2d. 198, 209 (Wis. 1961).

38 100 ALR2d 1141, 1146, Public School Teacher—Dismissal (1965).

39 Wyatts v. School District No. 104, Fergus County, 417 P.2d 221, 224 (Mont. 1966).

SIX

The Protections of Teacher Tenure

Nearly 40 states have statewide teacher tenure laws. Although these laws vary somewhat, they all provide basic rights which help secure your position within the school district. Basically, as a tenured teacher, you may not be removed from your teaching position without specific or good cause. Furthermore, a dismissal cannot be an outright firing. Your school board must follow specific procedures, and if it does not, you are entitled to reinstatement and to any wages you would have earned.

Tenure laws have been developed for the protection of teachers. Even in the ten or so states which do not have tenure protections provided for all districts, over half have "spring notification" requirements. These laws apply to all teachers, and generally provide for an automatic renewal of a contract unless the teacher is otherwise notified by a certain date. Similar notification provisions apply to probationary teachers in many states which provide for tenure. For a basic statement of your state's tenure law, see the chart at the end of this chapter.

The reason tenure laws came into being was to ensure maintaining capable, experienced teachers by preventing their removal for personal or political reasons. Tenure laws act as a protection for academic freedom. If you have tenure, you cannot be arbitrarily dismissed, or dismissed for undisclosed or disguised reasons. As one court explained:

> [T]he broad purpose of teacher tenure is to protect worthy instructors from enforced yielding to political preferences and to guarantee to such teachers employment after a long period of satisfactory service regardless of the vicissitudes of politics or the likes or dislikes of those charged with the administration of school affairs.[1]

This means that you are guaranteed employment indefinitely. That is, you are guaranteed employment unless you do something which causes the guarantee to be lifted.

Many people feel that all teachers should have this kind of protection. Frequently, new teachers with new ideas are among those most likely to need the protections of academic freedom. However, the idea of tenure is not to protect teachers as much as possible, but to aid in setting a criteria for distinguishing bad teachers from good. The ultimate purpose is to benefit the students, the educational profession, and the community. Requiring a probationary period in which the non-tenured teacher must prove himself does not seem unreasonable. To provide the non-tenured teacher no protection does seem unreasonable, however, and several states and courts have provided such a teacher with limited protections.

HOW TENURE WORKS

In most states, tenure can only be attained after successful completion of a probationary period. This period is generally three years and re-employment for a fourth year. Substitute teaching, intern teaching, student teaching and teaching under emergency or provisional credentials are usually not considered a part of this period. At the end of the designated period, some states provide automatic tenure. In other states, recommendation by the school superintendent, and affirmative action by the school board is required; however, non-action will not prevent your acquiring tenure. A few states provide that the provisional period may be extended for a teacher whose work has been unsatisfactory. During this extended probation, he is given additional aid and supervision in an effort to improve the quality of his service.

Many laws also set forth continuing obligations which you must fulfill if you want to maintain your tenure status. The most notable obligation is that you continue your professional studies by taking graduate work in education or your major teaching subject. The continuing education requirements must be reasonable, and are generally limited in their extent. This obligation assures the schools that tenured teachers keep abreast of educational changes in their field. Where the obligation is reasonable, lack of compliance constitutes good cause for dismissal.

Tenured teachers have other obligations. For example, you must comply with the necessary changes within the school system. This means that if your school district has a serious financial problem and is forced to cut all teachers' salaries, your salary may also be cut, regardless of your tenure status. If you do not accept the cut. you may terminate your contract without being penalized, but you cannot sue for higher wages.

A cut in your salary is subject to some limitations. An assignment to a lower status, combined with a substantial cut in salary, may amount to a wrongful removal from your original position. This cannot be done without a just and substantial cause on the part of the school board. Even so, you are entitled to a hearing and may appeal the decision.

School boards usually have the power to transfer you if it is in the best interest of the efficient operation of the schools. However:

GUIDE
RULE
A TRANSFER MUST BE TO A POSITION WITHIN YOUR AREA OF CERTIFIED QUALIFICATION, OR THE AREA SPECIFIED IN YOUR CONTRACT. IT MUST ALSO BE TO A POSITION OF EQUAL PAY AND STATUS, AND IN THE SAME GENERAL LOCATION.

This means that you cannot be transferred to an unreasonable position, or to an inaccessible school. If you reject such a transfer, you cannot be dismissed for insubordination. Furthermore, you cannot be transferred from a tenured district to one of non-tenure without your consent.

Many states also provide that:

> Whenever a teacher who has acquired permanent status ... is promoted ... from a position of lower salary to one of higher salary, such teacher shall serve a probationary period ... in the higher position before acquiring permanent status therein, but shall retain the permanent status acquired in the lower position from which he or she was promoted.[2]

Therefore, if you attain tenure as a classroom teacher, you will be able to keep this permanent status, even though you are later promoted to an administrative position. You do not receive stepped-up tenure immediately upon appointment to the higher position. This also means that a teacher in a non-tenured area may be returned to his tenured one.

You may voluntarily relinquish tenure by resigning. Even if you later are employed by the same district, you must generally complete a new probationary period. However, if you are coerced into resigning, this will not affect your right to regain your tenure. Tenure also terminates upon retirement age, which is 65 in most states.

DISMISSAL PROCEDURES WHICH THE SCHOOL BOARD MUST FOLLOW

Once you have attained the status of tenure, you are entitled to its protections, most notably:

**GUIDE
RULE**

1. YOU MAY NOT BE DISMISSED OR REFUSED RENEWAL OF YOUR CONTRACT EXCEPT FOR CAUSES SET FORTH IN THE STATUTES, OR FOR "GOOD CAUSE."
2. THE SCHOOL BOARD MUST FOLLOW PROPER PROCEDURES IN DISMISSING YOU. IF IT FAILS TO DO SO, THE DISMISSAL IS INVALID, AND YOU ARE ENTITLED TO RENEWAL OF YOUR CONTRACT OR DAMAGES.

The "causes" for which a tenured teacher may be dismissed are set forth and discussed in Chapter Five on teachers' contracts.

In a few states, the board has the power to set up its own dismissal procedures. Nevertheless, it must still comply with the rudiments of due process, and the procedure used must not be inconsistent with applicable state laws. As a result, there is a great deal of uniformity in this area, and the following dismissal procedure is either the same or similar to the procedure required in your state:

DISMISSAL PROCEDURE

Suspension:

If your school principal has reason to believe it is necessary for the best interests and proper functioning of the school, you may be temporarily suspended without a hearing. The allowable period is usually five days, and most states provide that you are entitled to your salary during this period. If desired, dismissal proceedings must be initiated during this period or you must be reinstated. *For a tenured teacher, the dismissal procedures required for termination of a contract during the term are the same as the procedures required if the school board intends to consider non-renewal of your contract.* (This procedure is also required in most states for the dismissal *during the contract term* of a non-tenured teacher, but not where merely non-renewal of his contract is in issue.)

Recommendation to Terminate:

If it is believed that *cause* exists which would justify your dismissal, written notice is filed by the superintendent, or sometimes the school principal, with the school board. This notice recommends termination and states the evidence on which the recommendation is based.

Investigation.

A great majority of the states provide that the school board handles the hearing and all of the procedures involved. (Many people feel that the board cannot be impartial in deciding the issues, and as a result, several states have provided for the hearing to be handled by others, who in turn make a recommendation to the board. These new laws are discussed in this chapter in the section entitled, "An Impartial Hearing.") An investigation of the complaint is often made by the school board. Usually, the board has the school superintendent or principal interview teachers and students, and in general do the investigating.

Notice to You:

If the board determines that good cause probably exists which makes it desirable to consider termination or non-renewal of your contract, it must furnish you with written notice of intent to dismiss. This notice must be informative, and must clearly tell you that your proposed discharge is to be considered at a designated time and place, at which you will be given an opportunity to answer the charges. This notice must state the reasons for the proposed dismissal. Merely stating the statutory cause is insufficient; the testimony and evidence giving rise to such cause must be summarized. In other words, the notice must be sufficiently specific to allow you to prepare to meet the allegations.

A few states (e.g. California) and individual school districts provide that you must receive advance notice (90 days) of any teaching deficiencies. This is intended to provide you with an opportunity to correct any remedial deficiencies.

Right to a Hearing:

Tenured teachers have a right to a hearing on dismissal or non-renewal for cause. You must request a hearing within a set time limit or you are deemed to have waived the right. This time limit normally is stated in the notice you receive, and is generally between 15 and 20 days. If you feel that the notice you received was inadequate, demand proper notice before you participate in the hearing; otherwise, you are deemed to have waived any defects in notice. The school board will set a date for a hearing if such a date was not specified in the notice you received.

Preliminary Evidence:

Any evidence which the school board has is generally put on file for you or your attorney's inspection. All of this evidence may be used at the hearing. This means, however, that you may cross-examine opposing witnesses on statements they made in the preliminary evidence, as well as on any testimony they give at the hearing.

Witnesses:

You may subpoena any witnesses or evidence you will need or desire to have at the hearing.

General Nature of the Hearing:

The hearing is basically a formal process. Its main purpose is to allow you to offer evidence and reasons as to why you should not be terminated. The school board must act in good faith in attempting to provide a fair and impartial hearing. The hearing must not be provided merely to announce a prior decision that you have been dismissed; it must be to help the board make a fair and impartial decision.

The Hearing:

The hearing consists of a formal presentation of evidence, and you are given a chance to fully reply to the charges made against you. There is some variation on the formal elements, but most hearings will provide the following safeguards:

THE HEARING'S PROCEDURAL SAFEGUARDS

Right to Counsel—You have a right to be represented by an attorney or your educational union or association. The school board almost always is represented by their attorney.

Testimony of Witnesses Is Given Under Oath—All witnesses are sworn and administered an oath.

Right to Cross-Examine Opposing Witnesses—You have a right to cross-examine witnesses on any testimony they give at the hearing, and on any statements they made in the preliminary evidence. You may impeach the testimony of the opposing witnesses by showing an unworthy reputation for truth and veracity, or by showing bias or prejudice.

You May Introduce Evidence on Your Behalf—You have a right to introduce witnesses or evidence on your own behalf.

You have a right to present any evidence which tends to show that the charges against you are not bona fide, but are really a cover up for bias or violation of your constitutional rights.

Restriction of Evidence—You and the superintendent are generally allowed to present only that evidence which pertains to the charge of misconduct of which you were given notice. Only evidence which is trustworthy should be admitted, but there are few formal rules of evidence. Hearsay is allowed in many circumstances.

Burden of Proof—The burden of proof is on those who are trying to dismiss you. They do not have to prove beyond a reasonable doubt, but only by a "fair preponderance of the evidence." The evidence is sufficient where the alleged facts are established and reasonable inferences may be drawn.

A great deal of discretion is given to the board. The main limitation is that the board's decision must rest on evidence presented at the hearing, not on the board members' personal knowledge of the case, suspicion or speculation.

Stenographic Transcript of the Proceedings—A written record of the hearing is required, in order to facilitate appeal and review.

Written Decision—The school board must make a written decision. This decision must state the cause for the dismissal, if that is the result, and the evidence on which the board relied to support it. Decision of dismissal must be supported by a vote of at least a majority of the entire board.

Resignation—If you intentionally, deliberately and voluntarily resign before, during or after the hearing, and your resignation is accepted by the board, it is final. However, if your resignation was due to duress or threats by the school board, it is voidable.

Review of Dismissal Proceedings:

All states provide for some form of review, but the appeal procedures vary greatly among the states. Some states provide for direct appeal to the courts, while some provide for appeal to a state public employee relations board. Still others provide for combinations of these. On appeal, the reviewer will check to see if the proper procedure was followed, if it was fair, and if the decision was supported by the evidence.

AN IMPARTIAL DECISION

Due process requires that you be treated fairly. Fairness requires notice, an opportunity to be heard, and a decision made by an impartial board. But how can the school board always render an impartial decision? Certainly the board tries to be open-minded, but the difficulty arises from its dual characteristic as both judge and prosecutor.

Oftentimes the board cannot help but be pressured. The board hired the superintendent, the administrators, and most of the witnesses who claim that cause exists for your dismissal. The board feels it must trust the judgment and discretion of these people and demonstrate confidence in their decisions. Also, the members of the school board are subject to popular prejudice and pressure because they are elected officials. Although the community is often passive about the running of the schools, it may well become upset over a controversial teacher and demand his removal. This cannot be allowed, particularly if the controversy arose because the teacher was merely exercising his constitutional right of free speech, political activity, etc. The board hopefully would try to be impartial, but the difficulty is obvious, especially in close cases. As a result, the school board should be freed of these pressures.

New Laws:

Several states have helped to provide for impartial decisions by enacting laws which do not require the school board to judge the facts and validity of the charges. California, for example, provides for transfer of the tenure hearing to the courts. The court conducts the hearing, determines the truth of the charges, and decides on the merits.[3] Colorado provides for a hearing before a panel composed of one member selected by the teacher, one by the school board, and one by the other two.[4] New Jersey, on the other hand, provides for a state official to conduct the hearing, and make the factual determination.[5]

Oregon's teacher dismissal statute is among the most progressive. This statute is entitled the Fair Dismissal Law.[6] It provides that if the district superintendent believes a "permanent teacher" no longer is benefiting the system, or should be dismissed for cause, the superintendent can suspend the teacher. Within five days, the teacher must be reinstated with no loss of pay, or dismissal proceedings must be instituted.

Twenty days before the superintendent makes his recommendation for dismissal to the board, he must notify the teacher of his intention, the grounds on which the recommendation is based, and a concise statement of the facts. He also sends a notice to the school board and to what is termed the "Fair Dismissal Appeal Board."

The teacher or the school district may then ask for advisory assistance from a Professional Review Committee, which is a panel of three members appointed by the State Superintendent of Public Instruction. This panel will assist the teacher, the superintendent and the school board in resolving the problem.

If the school board approves the dismissal, the teacher has five days to appeal to the "Fair Dismissal Appeals Board." This board consists of four members appointed by the Governor; one member is a school administrator, one a teacher, one a member of a school board, and one is not associated with any school district. This appeals board will then conduct a formal hearing similar to the kind previously discussed.

The decision of the Fair Dismissal Appeals Board is final. The only recourse from this decision is a hearing to see if the entire dismissal procedure was followed according to law. As you can see, this procedure guarantees to the teacher a hearing by an impartial "judge."

New Ideas:

The number of states which have acted to assure you of an impartial hearing are relatively few in number, but there are several self-help procedures which your teacher's organization could seek to have instituted:

1. One way the school board could help to insulate itself from preconceived opinions would be to separate its functions. The administrators could notify the teacher of the intent not to renew the teacher's contract. The two parties could then meet together and discuss the reasons. If the administrators still felt the same, they could submit their recommendation and the reasons for it to the school board. The board could then set a hearing, and this would be the first time it heard either side.

2. The hearing could be held before an independent hearing examiner, who would make findings and recommendations to the board. The board still has control of the final decision, but this would reduce the possibility of partiality. The only problem is that, in many states, the board does not have the power to provide for such a procedure.

DUE PROCESS RIGHTS OF NON-TENURED TEACHERS

The probationary teacher has few of the procedural or substantive protections which are granted to tenured teachers. A probationary teacher has a short-term contract which the school board does not have to renew. Most courts feel that renewal may be refused without notice, a hearing or good cause. This is often most inequitable. For example, in those few states which do not provide for tenure, would it be right to allow a teacher who has been in the district for 15 years to be dismissed without granting him a hearing, or explaining the reasons? He may believe that non-renewal was because he had exercised his constitutional rights, or he may suspect false gossip about his private life or teaching techniques. Maybe he just wants to know why. The courts have begun to show some concern for protecting non-tenured teachers' rights.

Non-tenured teachers have always had one main protection—their contract. As a general rule, in the absence of statutory or contractual provisions stating that the teacher may be dismissed at any time at the pleasure of the school board (and this is rarely the case):

GUIDE **RULE**	A TEACHER EMPLOYED UNDER A VALID CONTRACT MAY NOT BE DISCHARGED WITHOUT JUSTIFIABLE *CAUSE* BEFORE THE END OF THE TERM OF THE CONTRACT.

If it is believed that cause exists, most states, including California and New York, require that you be granted all of the substantive and procedural protections required for the dismissal of a tenured teacher. As a Massachusetts statute provides, due process requires:

> [A non-tenured teacher] ... who has been teaching for more than ninety days, shall not be dismissed for any reason unless at least fifteen days, exclusive of customary vacation periods, prior to the meetings at which the vote is to be taken, he shall have been notified of such intended vote and, if he so requests, he shall have been furnished by the committee with a written statement of the cause or causes for which the dismissal is proposed and if he so requests, he has been given a hearing before the school committee at which he may be represented by counsel, present evidence and call witnesses to testify in his behalf and examine them, and the superintendent shall have given the committee his recommendation thereon.[7]

This law applies to suspension and dismissal during the school year, but not to non-renewal of a contract.

Non-renewal of a contract incurs certain detriments that are not unlike being dismissed. If your contract is not renewed, it is harder to find a job; and, if you are married or have a family, there will be added difficulties in relocating in a distant district. Therefore, some protections should exist for non-tenured teachers. Not many states are willing to extend tenure protections to probationary teachers. This means that you must look for better contract agreements, negotiation demands, and possibly court decisions that will favor your teaching position.

Some courts have shown a willingness to provide non-tenured teachers with some limited protections. For example, in one case a teacher's contract was not renewed after she had taught in a non-tenured district for 12 years. For several months prior to her non-renewal, the teacher had taken an active part in the civil rights movement. The court said that the reasons the school board gave for the dismissal were unsupported in fact, and were mere subterfuge for infringement upon this teacher's constitutional rights.[8] The court set forth the rule that the school board may exercise great discretion in its hiring and firing of non-tenured teachers, but "[d]iscretion means the exercise of judgment, not bias or capriciousness. Thus it must be based upon fact and supported by reasoned analysis."[9]

In addition, you may not be refused renewal of your contract for violation of an unannounced board policy. You do not have to guess as to what is acceptable conduct or speech. Therefore:

<table>
<tr><td>GUIDE
RULE</td><td>REASONS FOR NON-RENEWAL ARE INVALID IF THEY ARE PATENTLY ARBITRARY, WHOLLY UNSUPPORTED IN FACT, BASED ON A VIOLATION OF AN UNANNOUNCED POLICY, OR VIOLATE YOUR CONSTITUTIONAL RIGHTS.</td></tr>
</table>

It is often argued that teachers have no way of knowing whether or not the reasons for non-renewal violate this rule, when the school board has no duty to explain the reasons or to grant a hearing. A few states, including Alaska and California, therefore, provide that even non-tenured teachers have a right to a statement of the reasons for non-renewal, and an informal hearing. This does not put a great burden on school boards, nor does it lead to much involvement in legal disputes, because the decision of the school board in such a hearing is generally conclusive. This kind of procedure merely requires the board to show that a valid reason, based on sufficient evidence, exists, which makes the retention undesirable. The *burden is on you* to show that the reason is not substantiated.

Since only a very few states provide these protections by statute, non-tenured teachers must generally look to the courts for protection. Some authority exists to the effect that a non-tenured teacher may request and be granted a hearing which will provide minimum due process protections. At this hearing, he has the burden of proving he has been wronged, since the school board may base its decision on any valid reason or, if uncontested, on no reasons at all. Such was the decision of a 1970 case involving a first year university professor whose contract was not renewed.[10] In this case, the teacher believed that the real reason for non-renewal of his contract was based on his having exercised his First Amendment rights. The court said that a non-tenured teacher's minimum rights to due process include:

1. A statement of reasons for non-renewal, furnished on request, and
2. Notice of a hearing at which he may respond to the reasons, upon request.

The court further stated that:

> At such a hearing, the professor must have a reasonable opportunity to submit evidence relevant to the stated reasons. The burden of going forward and the burden of proof rests with the professor. Only if he makes a reasonable showing that the stated reasons are wholly inappropriate as a basis for decision or that they are wholly without basis in fact would the university administration become obliged to show that the stated reasons are not inappropriate, or that they have a basis in fact.[11]

Four days later, the same court decided a case involving two public school teachers who had been teaching in a non-tenured school district for six and 18 years respectively, and were notified that non-renewal of their contracts had been recommended.[12] The teachers in this case alleged that the board's decision not to renew their contracts was without reason, without basis in fact, and without procedures which would help provide for a fair, rational decision. The court agreed that all teachers are protected against a non-renewal decision which is not supported in fact or on reasoned analysis, as well as against a decision which is based on a violation of the teacher's constitutional rights. The court then set forth the procedure which it felt was necessary in order to provide non-tenured teachers with minimum due process protection:

> ... [A] teacher in a public elementary or secondary school is entitled to a statement of the reasons for considering non-renewal, a notice of a hearing at which the teacher can respond to the stated reasons, and the actual holding of such a hearing if the teacher appears at the specified time and place .... [T] he Board's ultimate decision may not rest on a basis of which the teacher was never notified, nor may it rest on a basis to which the teacher had no fair opportunity to respond.[13]

Even under these two cases, the school board might not be required to provide written notification of the reasons for non-retention and, as one court stated:

> ... [W] here the only matter in issue is a difference of view over a school board's exercise of judgment and discretion concerning matters non-constitutional in nature, the board is not required to conduct a hearing.[14]

Many of the cases discussed in Chapter Four on your constitutional rights involved non-tenured teachers. As that chapter suggests, the courts will discern the real reasons for your dismissal and will grant you relief if the reasons constitute a violation of your rights.

It must be stressed that not all courts are willing to grant non-tenured teachers the right to a statement of reasons for non-renewal and a chance to refute them at an informal hearing. In fact, only a minority of courts are presently willing to do so—but it is a rapidly growing minority. The courts and state legislatures are becoming increasingly concerned about your rights, and they have shown an increasing willingness to grant you the right to due process procedures where it is proper. As the number of qualified teachers grows, school boards have a greater ability to initially select good teachers. As a result, it is no overbearing burden to require the board to grant these highly qualified but non-tenured teachers a chance to respond to the reasons for their removal.

PINPOINTING THE PROTECTIONS OF TENURE

Tenure is an employment security device which provides you with two main protections: (1) removal from your job may be based only on reasons constituting "cause"; and (2) specific dismissal procedures must be followed by the school board.

Where you, as a tenured teacher, are to be terminated for cause, minimum procedural due process requires that:

1. You be notified of the reasons for your termination in sufficient detail to fairly enable you to respond to the charges;
2. You be informed of the names of the witnesses against you, and the nature of their testimony;
3. At a reasonable time after such notice, you must be granted an opportunity to be heard in your own defense; and
4. The hearing must be conducted in such a manner that a fair and impartial decision will be rendered.

The exact particulars of the notice and hearing requirements are set up in your state statutes. They vary in content somewhat, but all of them provide for these minimum safeguards.

Due process requires a fair and impartial decision. The school board is under a great many pressures, and as a result, an impartial decision in *all* cases is not feasible. Several states have enacted procedures which relieve the school board of the duty to conduct the hearing and make the findings of fact. It is likely that many more states and individual school boards will make an effort to set up procedures which will fully assure you of a fair and impartial hearing.

Non-tenured teachers have few of the protections provided tenured teachers. As a general rule, the school board may dismiss a non-tenured teacher whenever it, in good faith, believes it will benefit the school system. There are some limitations to the school board's authority to dismiss, however.

1. Dismissal of a non-tenured teacher during the term of his contract is allowed only where cause exists and the statutory dismissal procedure is followed. In essence, the same protections guaranteed tenured teachers are granted to non-tenured teachers when the dismissal is before the end of the contract's term.
2. The school board may not base its decision of non-renewal of a non-tenured teacher's contract on reasons which are patently arbitrary, wholly unsupported in fact, based on a violation of an unannounced policy, or that violate your constitutional rights.

Non-tenured teachers also have a right to notice of non-renewal by a specific date. If you are not notified by that date that your contract is not to be renewed, you should write and send notice to the school board that you accept the next year's contract.

Most states and courts have yet to guarantee non-tenured teachers a right to a statement of the reasons for non-renewal and a hearing upon request. Such protections would help to assure non-tenured teachers that their dismissal was not based on prohibited reasons. Only a minority of state legislatures and courts have granted teachers within their jurisdiction these rights, but it is an increasing minority.

STATES HAVING STATE-WIDE TENURE LAWS, JANUARY 10, 1971

The following states have tenure laws governing all districts. Most states require teachers to serve a probationary period of several years plus re-employment for a following year. Most states also provide that if the school board is considering non-renewal of a teacher's contract, notice must be given by a certain date. If no notice is given by that date, your contract is considered renewable upon your acceptance. The notice requirement generally applies to ALL teachers, tenured and non-tenured. Not all laws refer to a notification date for tenured and non-tenured teachers, however.

State	Probationary Period	Date for Notice of Non-renewal
Alabama	3 years	Last day of the term
Alaska	2 years	Last day of the term; for a tenured teacher - March 16.
Arizona	3 years	March 15th
Arkansas	None, but annual contracts for up to 3 years may be alternatively used.	Within the contract term or 10 days after end of school year.
Colorado	3 years	April 15th
Connecticut*	3 years (3-6 mos. in Bridgeport)	March 1
Delaware	3 years	May 1
District of Col.	2 years	– –
Florida†	3 yrs. - may be extended to 4 yrs.	At least 4 weeks before end of year.
Hawaii	2 years - may be extended for up to 5 years.	– –
Idaho	2 years	March 1
Illinois	3 yrs. in Chicago; 2 yrs. in districts of less than 500,000 population.	60 days prior to term's end
Indiana	5 years	May 1
Iowa	None	April 10
Kentucky	4 years	May 15
Louisiana	3 years	– –
Maine	3 years	6 mos. prior to contract's end for tenured teachers.
Maryland	2 years - no specific period in Baltimore City.	May 1
Massachusetts	3 years	April 15

State	Probationary Period	Date for Notice of Non-renewal
Michigan	2 years; may be extended to 3.	60 days before the close of school.
Minnesota+	2 years; 3 years in Duluth, Minneapolis and St. Paul.	April 1
Missouri	5 years; 3 years in St. Louis	April 15
Montana	3 years	April 1 for tenured teachers; not specified for non-tenured.
Nevada	2 years	April 1
New Hampshire	Not referred to, but specific rights after 3 years.	March 15
New Jersey	3 years	– –
New Mexico	3 years	Before the closing day of school
North Dakota	Not mentioned	April 15
Ohio	3 to 5 years	April 30
Oklahoma	Not referred to, but hearing rights after 3 years.	April 10
Pennsylvania	2 years	10 days notice after an unsatisfactory rating in the bi-annual ratings.
Rhode Island	3 years	March 1
South Dakota	Not mentioned, but after 2 yrs. teachers have a right to notice on non-renewal.	April 1 for teachers having served for 2 years.
Tennessee	3 years	30 days before end of school year.
Virginia	3 years	April 15
Washington	None	April 15
West Virginia	3 years	April 1 for tenured teachers
Wyoming	3 years	March 15

* Special local tenure laws in Bridgeport, Hartford, New Britain, New Haven, Stanford and Waterbury.

† Duval, Hillsborough and Volusia Counties have special local tenure laws.

+ Tenure provisions differ in Duluth, Minneapolis and St. Paul.

STATES HAVING NEARLY FULL STATE-WIDE TENURE

	Extent of Tenure	Probationary Period	Notice Date
California	Tenure is state-wide, but is optional in districts with average daily attendance of less than 250 pupils.	3 yrs. in districts having 250 pupils. 2 yrs. in districts with 60,000 pupils.	May 15
New York	State-wide except for certain rural districts: In union free districts of over 4500 In city school districts . . . . In districts other than the above .	3 years 1 to 3 years Not to exceed 5 years	60 days prior to end of probationary period.
Texas	Optional in all school districts	3 years - may be extended to 4.	April 1

STATES HAVING TENURE IN CERTAIN PLACES ONLY,
SPRING NOTIFICATION, OR ANNUAL OR LONG-TERM CONTRACTS

	Tenure in Certain Places Only	Continuing Contract Law of Spring Notification Type	Annual or Long-term Contracts
Georgia	DeKalb, Fulton and Richmond Counties provide for tenure after 3 years probation.		Annual contracts in all districts except for the 3 tenure counties.
Kansas	Kansas City, Topeka and Wichita (cities having a population over 120,000). 3 year probation period.	Other districts provide for continuing contracts unless notice of non-renewal is given by March 15.	
Mississippi	No tenure laws		Long-term contracts permitted for up to 3 years.
Nebraska	Lincoln and Omaha. 3 yrs. probation, may be extended 1-2 yrs. Notice required by April 1.	Non-tenured areas provide for contract renewal unless notice is given by April 15.	
No. Carolina	No tenure laws	Notice must be given prior to close of the year, if a contract is not to be renewed.	
Oregon	"Permanent teacher" status and rights are granted after 3 years probation to teachers in districts of 4500 or more students or where tenure was in effect on Aug. 24, 1965.	All non-tenured teachers have a right to notification by March 15 if their contract is not to be renewed.	
So. Carolina	No tenure laws		No statutory requirements on length of contract term. Annual contracts are generally used.
Utah	No tenure laws		Contracts cannot exceed 5 years.
Vermont	No tenure laws		Annual contracts are generally used, but there are no provisions in the law as to permissible length.

	Tenure in Certain Places Only	Continuing Contract Law of Spring Notification Type	Annual or Long-term Contracts
Wisconsin	Tenure is limited to Milwaukee City and County, 3 years probation.	Non-tenured teachers are entitled to spring notification of non-renewal of their contracts, by April 1.	

For a more thorough explanation of your state's tenure provisions, see "Teacher Tenure and Contracts," National Education Association Research Report 1971-R3

FOOTNOTES

1 School District No. 8, Pinal County v. Superior Court, 433 P.2d 28, 30 (Ariz. 1967).
2 La. Rev. Stat. 17.463 (Cum. Supp. 1970).
3 Cal. Educ. Code § 13412-13 (1960).
4 Colo. Rev. Stat. Ann. § 123-18-17 (1968).
5 New Jersey Teacher Employees Hearing Act; New Jersey Stat. Ann. § 18A: 6-10 (1960).
6 O.R.S. § § 342.805 to 342.955 (1971).
7 Mass. Laws, chapter 388 § 1 (1970), amending chapter 71 § 42.
8 Johnson v. Branch, 364 F.2d 177 (4th Cir. N.Car. 1966), cert. denied, 385 U.S. 1003 (1967).
9 Id. at 181.
10 Roth v. Board of Regents of State Colleges, 310 F.Supp. 972 (U.S. Dist. Ct. Wis. 1970).
11 Id. at 980.
12 Gouge v. Joint School District No. 1, 310 F.Supp. 984 (U.S. Dist. Ct. Wis. 1970).
13 Id. at 992.
14 Lucas v. Chapman, 430 F.2d 945, 947 (5th Cir. Miss. 1970).

SEVEN

Following Appropriate Grievance Procedures

Over the years, teaching has become increasingly more complex. Teachers squarely face today's social problems. They teach courses and concepts which have never been taught in the past. They have necessarily become more competent, professional and specialized. Realizing this, teachers feel that they need and deserve to play a greater role in determining salary increases and working conditions.

Newer and stronger demands for better working conditions are being made by teachers. As one writer described this "teacher militancy":

> No Madison Avenue campaign has ever changed a client's image as radically as the nation's teachers have changed theirs. Kindly Mr. Chips and modest schoolmarm have been wiped off the public mind. Tough union leaders and equally tough spokesmen for the once soft-spoken National Education Association and its local affiliates leave no doubt that their mission is not to get a charitable apple for their teachers but to bring home the bacon of new pay scales and power over school policy.[1]

To present effectively and gain accessions to demands, proper procedures must be followed. Teachers generally have no desire to strike or to get caught up in labor-management problems. They want to teach. However, their awareness of many of the system's shortcomings and their interest in the upgrading of the profession has influenced teachers to seek bilateral control over terms and conditions of employment and educational policy. Teachers are professionally as well as personally concerned. Their knowledge and concern should be recognized as an invaluable resource for school boards.

HOW TO MAKE YOUR RECOMMENDATIONS AND GRIEVANCES HEARD

To insure that your recommendations and grievances are heard, grievance procedures have been set up through state laws and by local school districts. There are basically three types of grievance procedures:

1. Internal grievance procedures. These procedures are generally used to present your personal problems or complaints.
2. Collective bargaining. These are procedures sometimes prescribed by statute, which provide a negotiating process for the settlement of disputes between the school board and teachers. Although these laws are not in force in all states, they have had a profound effect on all teachers, and similar procedures will eventually be used throughout the country.
3. Statutory grievance procedures. In some instances the law provides the procedures that must be followed. This is especially applicable if the dismissal of a teacher is involved. These procedures are thoroughly covered in the chapter on tenure.

In a broad sense, grievance means a complaint involving a work situation. It could also mean that there has been a violation, misrepresentation, or inequitable application of any contract or board policy provision. You may have a complaint about anything from the amount of your salary, or "extra duties" which have been forced upon you, to an imposition on your teaching methods. In one case, for example, a teacher taught high school college prep chemistry courses. During one year, 6 per cent of his 67 students received A's, 12 per cent B's, 30 per cent D's, and 13 per cent F's. Parents complained to the principal about the grading system. The principal observed that for the past three years, the grade distribution did not conform to marks received by college prep students in other classes, and from other teachers. The principal ordered the teacher to revise his marking system to "bring it into line with the marks received by college preparatory students in other classes in the school." Failure to comply would be regarded as "an act of insubordination." The teacher filed a grievance under the collective bargaining contract between the school and the teacher's association. The arbitrator ruled that the way a teacher evaluates and grades his students is a condition of employment, and since the teacher had followed his method for nearly ten years, he did not have to comply with the principal's order.[2]

Grievance procedures are especially important because.

1. They help you to resolve quickly and equitably, at the lowest possible administrative level, problems you may have in relation to established personnel policies. They help you to avoid delayed remedial action, undesirable publicity and legal expenses which are sometimes incurred by taking your grievances to court.
2. In many instances, you cannot ask the court to provide a remedy for your problem unless you have followed the proper procedures provided by your school district

Even though the procedure may be of no use at its initial stages, if administrative review could possibly correct the errors, you must still follow it.

You are not required to exhaust administrative remedies before going to court, however, when school authorities themselves have ignored the legal procedure. For example, a teacher in Montana was discharged during her contract term without a regular or special meeting of the school board. This was held improper, and therefore the teacher was entitled to damages. The court so held even though the teacher had not followed the proper grievance procedures when it was impossible for the teacher to have a grievance hearing.[3]

LOCAL GRIEVANCE PROCEDURES

Local grievance procedures are based on the written policies of the board, which are often set forth in its booklet on certified staff policies. Most grievance procedures are formed within these basic guidelines:

1. *Definition of terms.* Terms such as "binding arbitration," "grievance," and "aggrieved" are clearly defined.
2. *Right to consultant.* You are given a right to be represented by a member of the grievance committee of your employee's association (local affiliates of the NEA, AFT, etc.) or an attorney, at each level of the procedure.
3. *Protection from reprisal.* You may not be "punished" in any way for initiating or participating in a grievance.
4. *Written records.* Records of formal proceedings are kept and made available to all parties.
5. *Sequential levels of grievance.* These will be discussed more thoroughly in the following pages. Every effort is and should be made to resolve your complaint through informal activities before formal procedures are used.
6. *Time periods for each level.* Maximum time periods to initiate and complete the action are indicated at each level of the procedure.
7. *Termination of grievance.* The procedures will terminate at any level when you indicate in writing that you wish to do so, or if you fail to pursue your complaint within the specified time limit.

When you have a personal complaint, you should make a sincere attempt to resolve it through informal communications with your principal before the complaint becomes formalized as a grievance.

If you are a member of the National Education Association or the American Federation of Teachers, you can count on their help in the filing and processing of your grievance. They often have grievance committees set up which will advise and counsel you, prepare and evaluate your case, and, in some instances, handle the grievance in their name and thereby incur all of the expenses and inconvenience which may be involved. Some of the personnel policies of school districts establish that such employee organizations have the responsibility of processing the grievances of non-member educators within the district, as well as of those who are members of the association.

If you fail to satisfactorily resolve your complaint informally, you should follow your school's established grievance procedures. These procedures attempt to secure, at the lowest possible administrative level, equitable solutions to your problems. When you cannot solve your problem by merely talking to the principal, you are required to file a written grievance if you want redress. The sample form shown in Exhibit 3 will effectively serve as a form for filing your complaint:

SAMPLE FORM FOR FILING A GRIEVANCE

Name of complainant .... Date of filing ....
Home address ....
Home telephone .... No. of years in school district ....
Position held ....
Name and address of school ....
Principal .... School telephone ....
Grievance representative (i.e., NEA or AFT representative if you have one) ..
....
Provision of school policy allegedly violated ....
....
Statement of grievance ....
....
Action requested ....
....

....
Signature of complainant

EXHIBIT 3

Most school districts provide for five sequential levels in their grievance procedures. Once you have written up your complaint, you must file it with your immediate supervisor. This is always the first level in local grievance procedures. In some schools, the immediate supervisor with authority to act will be the head of your department, but in others he will be the school principal. The supervisor must then review your complaint and communicate his decision within a set number of days (Since five days is generally the specified number, it will be used as an example.) If you are dissatisfied with his decision, you have five days to appeal.

Your appeal is then taken to the superintendent's representative (in larger school districts) or to the superintendent himself. He will hear your complaint within a set number of days (usually ten). At this hearing, you are usually allowed to call witnesses. The representative or the superintendent will communicate his decision and the supporting reasons within five days. If you are still dissatisfied with the decision, you may appeal to the next level. This would be the superintendent in cases where your appeal had.been heard by his representative.

After your appeal is heard by the superintendent, many districts provide for advisory arbitration. The arbitration committee is generally composed of one person appointed by the superintendent, one person appointed by the complainant, and one person appointed by the two members already appointed. They will investigate all of the prior decisions, the reasons on which they were based, and any other relevant facts and data. Their advisory recommendation is then made to the superintendent, and a copy sent to you as complainant. Should this decision be unsatisfactory, you may appeal to the school board.

If you are not satisfied with the school board's decision, you may appeal to the final level. Many school districts provide for binding arbitration where all else has failed. The American Arbitration Association, or a mutually acceptable arbiter, is called upon to make the final decision. This decision is binding on all parties.

The proper grievance procedure is set forth in the diagram shown in Exhibit 4. This one is recommended by the Oregon State Board of Education. It is similar to those used in school districts throughout the country. Your local district's grievance procedure is probably either identical or very similar to this one. In Chicago, for example, the 1970 agreement between the Board of Education of the City of Chicago and the Chicago Teacher's Union provided for a grievance procedure which consisted of levels one, two (A), two (B), four and five.

Keep in mind that any decision pursuant to the grievance procedures shall be final and binding on you and the administration if it is not appealed to the next level. If it is appealed, the last level formulates the final decision unless otherwise provided by law. In cases involving dismissal or demotion, procedures already provided for under state tenure laws, or teacher dismissal laws, control.

It is always best to resolve your complaints informally. Talk your complaint over with the person(s) directly involved. This will help alleviate

FLOW CHART FOR GRIEVANCE PROCEDURES

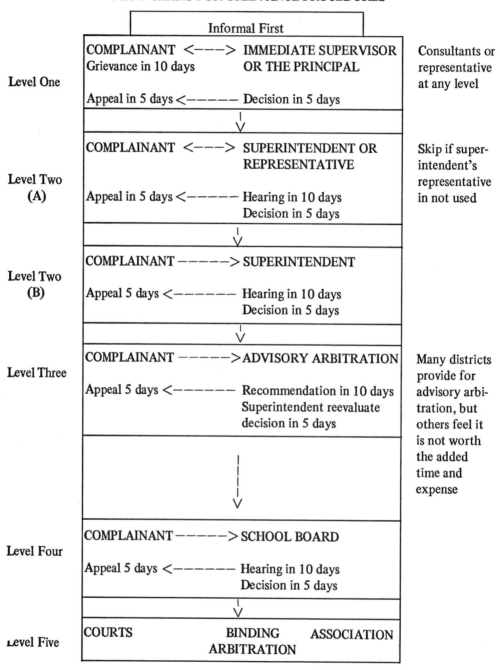

	Informal First	
Level One	COMPLAINANT <---> IMMEDIATE SUPERVISOR OR THE PRINCIPAL Grievance in 10 days Appeal in 5 days <----- Decision in 5 days	Consultants or representative at any level
Level Two (A)	COMPLAINANT <---> SUPERINTENDENT OR REPRESENTATIVE Appeal in 5 days <----- Hearing in 10 days Decision in 5 days	Skip if superintendent's representative in not used
Level Two (B)	COMPLAINANT -----> SUPERINTENDENT Appeal 5 days <----- Hearing in 10 days Decision in 5 days	
Level Three	COMPLAINANT -----> ADVISORY ARBITRATION Appeal 5 days <----- Recommendation in 10 days Superintendent reevaluate decision in 5 days	Many districts provide for advisory arbitration, but others feel it is not worth the added time and expense
Level Four	COMPLAINANT -----> SCHOOL BOARD Appeal 5 days <----- Hearing in 10 days Decision in 5 days	
Level Five	COURTS BINDING ASSOCIATION ARBITRATION	

EXHIBIT 4

some of the bitterness which sometimes results from the filing of grievances. If no solution results, you still have a right to file a formal written grievance.

STRIKES AND POSSIBLE REPERCUSSIONS

During the 1960's and early 1970's, the United States witnessed a growing discontent among teachers. This discontent was based on a number of factors, among them:

1. The amount of federal and state protection afforded private employees.
2. An increase in the number of employed public teachers.
3. Increased organization of teachers.
4. Consolidation of school districts.
5. Persistent low salaries during periods of inflation and economic prosperity.
6. Rivalry between the American Federation of Teachers and the National Education Association.
7. The influx of men into the profession.
8. The steady rise in the quality and educational attainment of teachers.

The first factor has had the strongest influence on teacher discontent. In 1935, the National Labor Relations Act gave workers in the private sector of employment the right to organize and to negotiate collectively on "wages, hours and other terms and conditions of employment."[4] Public employees were given no such protection, except for various insignificant civil service laws. Private employees had the power to force employers (i.e., through strikes) to improve their working conditions and wages, but public employees were denied the right to do the same. Teachers certainly had the right to discuss wages with their boards, but to "negotiate" suggests more than that. Negotiation is a means of imposing procedures which remove the school board's discretionary power as to whether or not to bargain over teacher demands, and it dictates responsibilities in the manner of response which the school board must make. Public employees want the same rights private employees have.

How can you exercise bilateral control over educational policy and the terms and conditions of employment? Private employees are able to exercise control over their wages and working conditions through unions and collective bargaining. One of the best influences in bargaining is the power to strike. It is now recognized that public employees also have the right to organize, and most states allow public employees to bargain collectively. You may belong to teachers' associations or unions without fear of reprisal by the school board. This right was stressed in a 1971 Virginia Federal Court case. In that case, a teacher caused a great deal of controversy in campaigning for the office of treasurer of the Virginia Education Association—so much so that the school board decided not to renew his teaching contract. However, the court said: "...a teacher may not be denied a teaching contract because of his actions in a professional association, regardless of how vigorous they are."[5]

GUIDE	ALTHOUGH MOST STATES GRANT TEACHERS THE RIGHT TO BARGAIN COLLECTIVELY, THE MOST INFLUENTIAL
RULE	MEANS OF APPLYING BARGAINING PRESSURE–THE RIGHT TO STRIKE–IS DENIED.

Teacher strikes are illegal in all but a very few states. Vermont, Hawaii and Pennsylvania allow public employees to strike, but only in limited situations. However, the fact that teacher strikes are illegal does not mean that they will not occur. In fact, strikes have continued to increase. There were 18 teacher strikes from 1953 to 1962, 46 from 1963 to 1966, and the rate continues to grow. When one notes the aversion most teachers feel toward striking, the figures clearly demonstrate the frustration and discontent that many feel. Teachers do not want to strike, but many feel forced to do so. As the Research Division of the NEA disclosed:

> More than one-third of all public school teachers believe categorically that teachers should never strike. On the other hand, one-half of all teachers believe teachers should strike, but only under *extreme* conditions and after all other means have failed.[6]

Many teachers feel that they cannot demand respect for classroom rules and teach students the meaning of the law, and then walk outside and begin a strike in open defiance of state statutes. In addition, many teachers feel that a break in the flow of their lesson plans lowers the quality of education that they can provide their students.

What Is a Strike?

In August of 1968, teachers in a Michigan school district had not yet signed their contracts. They voted to "withhold" their services, maintaining that, since no contracts were signed, they were not yet public employees and were, therefore, not on strike. The court found that a continuing employment relationship existed, such that absence from work constituted an illegal strike.[7] *A strike,* as this case suggests, *is any concerted refusal to work.*

Teachers have sought in various ways to force settlement of their demands without formally "striking." Mass resignations and various sanctions have occasionally been successful. Mass resignations involve the simultaneous submission of resignations by a significant number of teachers, in an effort to gain accession to their demands. Generally, the local teachers' organization supplies the teachers with uniform resignation forms, and either the individual teacher or the organization holds them. They are not necessarily handed in, but they act as a threat to the school board. Mass resignations have taken place on local, county and state levels. For example, in the late 1960's, over 25,000 of Florida's teaching force of 60,000 were involved in a mass resignation.

Most courts look on mass resignations as a strike, because it is a concerted work stoppage. In New York City, an impasse caused tenured teachers whose contracts had expired not to report to work on opening day. Their resignations had not been submitted to the school board but they were in the hands of the teachers' association. There was no obligation to work, and a lawful resignation could be submitted, but the court said it was up to the individual teacher to show that his resignation was in good faith and not meant to meet strike objectives.[8]

If mass resignations are considered valid, there is no obligation for you to return to your prior employment. However, should you do so, your tenure and seniority rights may be adversely affected because interruption of a continuous service can terminate your rights, unless your state statutes provide otherwise. If your state has no specific provisions as to how tenure is to be acquired and maintained, the school board would be able to grant return of your rights as a topic of settlement negotiations, and it would no doubt do so. At any rate, mass resignation is an extremely inadequate solution to the problems you may have.

Sanctions.

Sanctions were created by the NEA and, as employed, mean:

> ... censure, suspension or expulsion of a member; severance of relationship with an affiliated association or other agency; imposing a deterrent against a board of education or other agency controlling the welfare of the schools; bringing into play forces that will enable the community to help the board or agency to realize its responsibility; or the application of one or more steps in the withholding of services.[9]

In some cases, certain NEA sanctions have been held to constitute strikes, but generally they are not. Sanctions cause no violation of the contract, and there are many different forms. Sometimes sanctions result in NEA members refraining from negotiating for a new contract, and sanctions often seek to have teachers relocate from a "censured" district, or have new teachers stay away. Sanctions provide only limited benefits, and are not always adequate to achieve satisfactory results.

COLLECTIVE BARGAINING

Your demands differ significantly from those of private employees. Many of your demands are the result of your professional concern—your desire to provide students with the best possible education. You care about your students; and, after all, they are what school is all about. You have a special expertise. Being in school all day, and working closely with students, you know how the educational system can be improved. School administrators and teachers alike realize how much students and the educational process are benefited when teachers are able to exercise bilateral control over educational policy. The cost of unresolved agreements is far too high. It might cost the board the loss of competent employees, or foster low morale. On your side, there is a loss of community support if demands are unreasonable or are not fully understood. If solutions can be provided, no one would be happier than the teacher and administrators. Many new laws and ideas are being tried to provide such a solution.

In the early 1960's, "collective negotiations," a supposedly strikeless form of collective bargaining, began to take form. Its purpose was to balance the power between the teacher and the school board. Prior to this time, the school board had nearly unilateral power to determine the terms and conditions of employment. Now, although public employee bargaining power is still in its formative stages, a great majority of teachers are in states which provide some type of collective bargaining statutes, or are in school districts which provide systems for collective negotiations.

Collective bargaining has been defined as:

> ... the performance of the mutual obligation of the employer and the representative of the employees to meet at reasonable times and confer in good faith with respect to wages, hours, and other terms and conditions of employment, or the negotiation of an agreement, or any question arising thereunder, and the execution of a written contract, ordinance or resolution incorporating any agreement reached if requested by either party, but such obligation does not compel either party to agree to a proposal or require the making of a concession.[10]

Collective bargaining does not infringe on the sovereign power of the school board. As this definition states, collective bargaining does not compel the school board to give up its ultimate responsibility for making decisions. Only a technique of procedure is required. The board cannot merely say to you, "Here is our offer, take it or leave it." After good faith bargaining, the board can, however, put forth a final offer which it will then take to impasse. One court describes the five basic steps in the negotiation process generally required by all collective bargaining laws as:

NEGOTIATION PROCESS FOR COLLECTIVE BARGAINING

1. The negotiations team must be chosen. This may consist of an independent negotiator, or all or part of the governmental employer or a committee thereof.
2. The negotiator must be instructed with the facts and information necessary to meet his counterpart on the other side. Parameters of positions must be established. The final outcome will often depend on how much information a negotiator has about his limitations and authorizations and how he uses this information.
3. The negotiating teams need to discuss their proposals. If this is undertaken in good faith as the law requires, without posturing or improper demands, there is no reason why agreement cannot be reached on all issues. Even if an impasse is reached, there are many opportunities for resolution by mediation, fact finding and arbitration. This is essential, since in the public sector there is no right to strike.
4. When the negotiators reach tentative agreement on matters under discussion, the same is reduced to writing and is presented to employer and employees and the public for consideration, discussion and eventual ratification or rejection.
5. If approved or adopted, the tentative proposals become part of the Code governing the relationship between employer-employee.[11]

The first and fourth steps are generally public. The second and third steps are settled in private. And in order to be fair to the taxpayer, the fifth step is often taken at a board meeting open to the public.

The school board must feel a sense of urgency if it is to bargain fairly. The effectiveness of negotiations will therefore depend on the impasse machinery. An impasse occurs when neither party feels an agreement can be reached. The dispute then must follow the impasse procedures. The object is, of course, for you and the school board to reach agreement prior to this point. Therefore, to aid in resolving disputes, effective impasse machinery must:

1. Make both parties feel that if the dispute is submitted to impasse, they will fare equally. If neither party will have a stronger position if impasse is reached, they will bargain fairly in the beginning without waiting for the final stage.
2. At the same time, it must be an adequate substitute for the power to strike.

There are three basic types of impasse machinery: mediation, fact finding, and arbitration.

Mediation is an informal procedure, in which a third party attempts to ease relations between teachers and the school board. He acts as a means of communication, and although he sometimes proposes compromises, he mainly attempts to help the parties reach agreement on their own solutions. Some statutes provide for mediation (a) if either party asks for it; (b) if the Public Employee Relations Board orders it; or (c) if both parties seek it.

Fact finding is fairly formal, and amounts to a form of advisory arbitration. Under this procedure, hearings are conducted, evidence is presented, and the fact finding panel decides the "true" facts and makes public recommendations. Although these recommendations are not binding, they generate public opinion. Use of fact finding helps to prevent strikes, and experience shows that the fact finder's recommendations are usually accepted.

Binding arbitration may be set up in one of three ways:

1. You and the school board each pick a representative and a neutral third representative is chosen.
2. A professional arbitrator is chosen by agreement.
3. An outside body selects the arbitrator.

The arbitration committee listens to both sides of the dispute and makes recommendations. These recommendations are binding on both parties. Arbitration may be (a) voluntary, in which case both parties must have agreed to use this method of settling their disputes; or (b) compulsory, in states which have statutes requiring the parties at an impasse to arbitrate.

Of the three basic types of impasse machinery, binding arbitration appears to be the most adequate substitute for strikes because it equalizes your power with that of the board. However, there are a number of serious objections:

1. If the arbitrator settles the dispute, the school board is not making the ultimate decision, and therefore, public sovereignty is infringed upon.
2. Binding arbitration has a tendency to make collective bargaining at its initial stages ineffective.
3. It is often felt that it is undesirable to leave the question of public employees' salaries in the hands of someone who is not responsible to the public.

Regardless of the objections, binding arbitration has many desirable aspects, and is gaining wide acceptance. It is particularly effective and acceptable when used as a means for deciding disputes not involving the expenditure of money.

Fact finding might be more effective if it were set up to provide that, if the school board failed to follow the fact finder's recommendations, you could then, but only then, strike. Public opinion would be more favorable, and striking would be seen as a justifiable act. On the other hand, you would be wise to follow the fact finder's recommendations, since public opinion would be strongly against you if you failed to do so.

As you can see, there is no perfect solution. Public employee bargaining rights are still in their formative stages. Many states have begun changing their laws in an attempt to provide you with a better bargaining position. These laws are often quite complex. Your state law will vary from the laws of most of the other states, because of the many solutions being tried. Massachusetts, Michigan, New Jersey, New York and Wisconsin, for example, have statutes requiring school boards to share the policy-making authority with their employees' organizations. California and Minnesota give teachers the right to "meet and confer" with local school boards. Connecticut, Maryland, Rhode Island and Washington have laws guaranteeing teachers the right to organize and bargain collectively with school boards. Vermont, Pennsylvania and Hawaii allow strikes, but only when there is no clear and present danger to a sound educational policy, and when the public health, safety and welfare is not endangered.

The important thing to remember is that, because of the "new" desire to help public employees improve their bargaining position, these laws are constantly changing, and changing for the better. You will feel these changes every year. You will find that your demands and solutions to educational problems will play a greater role in the educational system.

As your bargaining position improves, it is possible that the education of your students will also improve. Higher salaries will keep quality teachers in the profession, and their spirit and morale will be high. Collective bargaining, as already used in many states, allows you to negotiate over such things as:

1. Grievance procedures.
2. The number and kind of extra-curricular duties you will be required to perform.
3. Textbook selection.
4. Curriculum design.
5. Pupil ratio and class size.
6. Instructional aids.
7. Compensation for extra-curricular activities.
8. Use of teacher facilities.
9. Teaching and non-teaching duties.
10. Determination of academic standards.
11. Selection of administrative personnel.
12. Salaries and fringe benefits.
13. Payment for unused sick leave upon separation.
14. Audio-visual aids and other teaching aids.

Not all collective bargaining agreements provide for negotiations over all of these items, or of the endless number not listed. However, many of them are covered, and as your bargaining power increases, so will the topics over which you may bargain.

SUMMARY

Grievance procedures are meant to benefit everyone. You should try to follow them. Local grievance procedures are set up to provide a process for the airing of your personal problems. If you cannot solve your problems informally, you may file a written grievance with your immediate supervisor. If he is unable to satisfactorily solve your complaint, you may appeal to the higher authorities. Hopefully, an adequate solution can be found without undue hard feelings, cost or publicity.

A strike is any concerted refusal to work. Strikes are illegal and, as such, subject you to possible criminal contempt proceedings. They also generate unfavorable publicity. For bargaining procedures to be effective and, at the same time, agreeable to teachers, they must provide such a balance of power that resolution at early bargaining stages will be encouraged, and they must provide an adequate substitute for the right to strike.

The legal argument has always been that bilateral control over educational policy and the terms and conditions of employment infringes on the school board's discretionary powers. Many new systems are being tried to help balance power over educational policy between you and the school board, while simultaneously protecting the board's discretionary powers and not permitting strikes. Collective bargaining is rapidly becoming a most effective procedure for the presentation of your demands. Collective bargaining laws require the school board to bargain in good faith by following a technique of procedure and, for the most part, the school board is able to retain its discretion. The final aim is to encourage resolution at the initial bargaining stages. This can only be accomplished through impasse procedures which provide equal bargaining power in the case of unsettled disputes.

You as well as the school board have a duty to bargain in good faith. It must be kept in mind that the school board faces two serious dilemmas: (1) In financial matters, the board must try to meet your salary, fringe benefits and working condition needs and, at the same time, save money for educational and operational services. (2) In the bilateral formulation of school policies and standards, the board must retain public trust and serve the community's interests while trying to satisfy your demands. Cooperation and understanding are needed on both sides, if bargaining procedures are to function properly. You, your administration and the school board will all benefit from such procedures and, more importantly, so will your students.

FOOTNOTES

1 Hechinger, "New Teacher Militancy," N.Y. Times, Sept. 9, 1967, at 19, col. 3 (city ed.).
2 Barnstable Teachers Association v. Barnstable School Committee Educators Negotiating Services, Dec. 2, 1968, case no. 1130-0043-68 (Fallon, Arbitrator); cited in 67 Mich. L. Rev. 1017, 1024-1025 (1967).
3 Wyatt v. School District No. 104, 417 P.2d 221 (Mont. 1966).
4 29 U.S.C. § 158 (d) (1964).
5 Lee v. Smith,_____ F. Supp. _____ (U.S. Dist. Ct. Vir., Jan. 5, 1971), quoted in Nolpe Notes, vol. 6, no. 3, p. 4 (March, 1971).
6 Nat'l Educ. Ass'n Jour., vol. 55, May, 1966, at 54.
7 School District for City of Holland v. Holland Education Association, 157 N.W.2d 206 (Mich. 1968).
8 Board of Education of City of New York v. Shanker, 283 N.Y.S.2d 432 (Sup. Ct., 1967).
9 Nat'l Educ. Ass'n, *Guidelines for Professional Sanctions* 9 (1963).
10 Mich. Comp. Laws Ann. §423.215 (1967).
11 Bassett v. Dade County Classroom Teacher's Association, Cir. Ct., 11th Judicial Cir., Dade Cy., Fla., # 71-1462 (March 25, 1971); quoted in Nolpe Notes, vol. 6, no. 6, p. 2 (June 1971).

EIGHT

The Authority of the School Board

The local board of education takes up one of the most important spaces in our educational system. It works with people, and its purpose is to assure its students the best possible education available within its financial spectrum. The school board is the representative of the people who govern the school. As such, the school board is generally a political body which is supposed to be non-partisan.

Teachers know about school boards, because they work under the policies, rules and regulations, as well as toward the educational goals, that the local board has established. Nevertheless, local boards have sometimes been considered aloof, in that there is frequently a lack of meaningful communication between teachers and their board. This lack of communication can be bridged by a better understanding of the board's rights, duties and powers.

School boards work under guidelines which establish and define their responsibilities. They have a Code of Ethics, and they follow specified procedures in obtaining their objectives. Their powers are broad in some areas, and limited in others. The local board makes a commitment to education, and implements that commitment through the district superintendent. He, in turn, works between teachers, administrators, and the board—all of whom are working for students.

WHAT IS A SCHOOL BOARD

You are hired by a board consisting of lay members in your community. Your local board of education is a governmental unit created by your state legislature. Each state has the responsibility of providing and maintaining an efficient school system for its students. The states carry out this responsibility through state boards or departments of education, and local school boards. The state department of education has the basic duties and responsibilities, and it sets the guidelines for the local boards to follow. Local boards must follow these guidelines, but they have a broad range of discretionary powers they may exercise in fulfilling their goal of running their local schools.

Your state department of education, among other things:

1. Authorizes textbook adoptions;
2. Authorizes courses of study for students;
3. Prescribes various rules and regulations for the general management of the schools;
4. Establishes state standards for public education. These standards are for elementary and secondary education. They tell what instruction is to be given in various fields, and what activities are to be provided.

Your local board of education derives its powers from the legislature and from the state board of education, not from the people. As stated in a book explaining to school board members the extent of their power:

> Since both the State Department of Education and the school district derive their powers from the Legislature, neither can increase or diminish its own powers.
>
> Nor can either encroach upon the powers of the other. Both exist at the pleasure of the Legislature which, in its discretion, can enlarge or decrease the powers of each.
>
> A board of education is provided in each district to manage and control the schools in that district. Although the members are appointed or elected within the district, it should be emphasized that boards of education perform a state function at a local level, and that their powers are derived not from the people of the district but from the Legislature.
>
> Boards of education can therefore perform only those acts for which some authority exists, expressly stated or implied, in the law or in the rules and regulations of the State Board of Education.[1]

What acts are proper for your local school board? Generally, the local board is not interfered with by the state board, so long as it follows the basic guidelines necessarily provided by the state board. If the state board approves, local districts may supplement or substitute course offerings or textbooks. Larger districts have curriculum specialists, and these persons usually set up programs which exceed the minimum requirements set up by the state board. Local districts are encouraged to go beyond the minimum standards set by the state board, because:

> The general purposes of the state requirements are to guarantee students a certain minimum educational opportunity, to provide for their physical

safety, and to also provide safety and equitable employment conditions to district employes. It is clearly *not* the state's intent to dictate every small detail of the day-to-day operation of the schools.[2]

This means that your local board has the powers necessary to carry out its everyday responsibilities. Their authority includes the right to:

1. Enforce the rules of the state board;
2. Hire employes and set wages so long as the wages are not below state requirements;
3. Determine the curriculum to be taught so long as it is not below the standards set by the state;
4. Provide and equip the district with the necessary materials for instruction and operation;
5. Enact rules and regulations governing the operation of the schools;
6. Enact reasonable rules and regulations governing students and employees;
7. Enforce discretionary decisions in order to carry out other duties and responsibilities assigned to school boards by the state.[3]

These powers are necessary if the school is to be run by the local board. The board itself answers to the state. The members of the board answer to the people in the community in which they live.

GUIDELINES FOR A MEMBER OF THE BOARD

Board members bear a heavy responsibility. Generally, they are in some sort of business other than education. A board member cannot be a professional employee (teacher, administrator) of the school board and still be a member. If that were the case, there would be a conflict of interests, and it would be very difficult for the member of the board to function without some bias. Members of the local board help run the schools and determine the quality of education that will be given to the students. The members of the board are volunteers who are concerned about education. They lead a team consisting of citizens in the community, school administrators, and classroom teachers. Their goal is to attain the best possible education, within limited resources, for children.

Your state sets up the legal qualifications necessary for a person to become a member of the board. These qualifications are by no means strict. Basically, the member must be able to read and write, have no contract or claim against the board, and he or she must be a resident for a certain period of time within the district.

These are the legal requirements, but there are also personal requirements which are desirable in a good board member. A member of the board must not use his position as a means of imposing his political philosophies on the schools. His position is non-partisan because his main purpose is to insure the best education for all students in the district. Political pressures will be brought upon him by members of the community, but these pressures must be weighed in light of their value to students, and not in light of personal interests or desires. This means that a board member must be intelligent, have integrity, be open-minded, and must have a strong interest in children and their welfare.

A member of the board should also know that:

> ..[A]school board, though a part of the executive rather than the legislative branch of the state's government, is, speaking strictly, neither executive nor legislative in its functions....It is concerned with the creation, under existing law, of school policies for the district, and for the evaluation of the effectiveness of these policies....[4]

In other words, the board sets policies, and the implementation of these policies is left to administrative channels within the school.

Similar to the Teacher's Code of Ethics is the Code of Conduct for board members. This code may vary in wording from state to state, but its intent and meaning are accepted throughout the country.

A typical Code of Conduct is set forth in Exhibit 5.

If a school board member works within such a Code of Conduct, he should be effective in his position. The Code explains what a good member should do. As the Code implies, and the guidebook states, some practices should be avoided:

> Experience has shown that board members lose effectiveness to the degree that they:
>
> 1. Interfere with the day-to-day routine details of school administration and supervision.
> 2. Refuse to support worthwhile school programs because of personal reasons.
> 3. Show favoritism to relatives or friends.
> 4. Make promises and commitments before the questions are fully discussed in the board meetings.
> 5. Join a clique to control board action.
> 6. Use board membership for political or business advancement for themselves, their families, their relatives, or their friends.
> 7. Indulge in petty criticism of the administration of their schools.
> 8. Divulge confidential information.
> 9. Assume authority in school matters when the board is not in session.
> 10. Accept gifts from school suppliers or contractors, or make personal purchases through the schools to gain advantage of the school discounts.[5]

A Code of Conduct

A School Board Member Should:

Understand that his basic function is "policy making" and not "administrative."

Discourage sub-committees of the Board *which tend to nulify* the board's policy making responsibility.

Refuse to "play politics" in either the traditional partisan, or in any petty sense.

Respect the rights of school patrons to be heard at official meetings.

Recognize that authority rests only with the Board in *official meetings*.

Recognize that he has no legal status to act for that Board outside of official meetings.

Refuse to participate in "secret" or "star chamber" meetings, or other irregular meetings which are not official and which all members do not have the opportunity to attend.

Refuse to make committments on any matter which should properly come before the Board as a whole.

Make decisions only after all available facts bearing on a question have been presented and discussed.

Respect the opinion of others and graciously accept the principle of "majority rule" in board decisions.

Recognize the superintendent should have full administrative authority for properly discharging his professional duties within limits of established board policy.

Act only after hearing the recommendations of the superintendent in matters of employment or dismissal of school personnel at an official meeting.

Recognize that the superintendent is the educational advisor to the board and should be present at all meetings of the board except when his contract and salary are under consideration.

Refer all complaints or problems to the proper administrative office and discuss them only at a regular meeting after failure of administrative solution.

Present personal criticisms of any school operation directly to the superintendent rather than to school personnel.

Insist that all school business transactions be on an ethical, and above board basis.

Refuse to use his position on a school board in any way, whatsoever, for personal gain or for personal prestige.

Refuse to bring personal problems into board considerations.

Advocate honest and accurate evaluation of all past employees when such information is requested by another school district.

Give the staff the respect and consideration due skilled professional personnel.

Adopted by
OREGON SCHOOL BOARDS ASSOCIATION

EXHIBIT 5

BOARD MEETINGS—PROCEDURES AND PURPOSES

In the meetings of the board, policies are formulated and decisions for school operations are made. Decisions cannot be made outside of a board meeting; therefore, procedure is very important.

The school board may hold a regular or special meeting. The meeting is public and you may attend in order to listen or to express your views. One of the most important aspects of a board meeting is the agenda. The agenda is usually prepared in advance and the meeting proceeds according to the schedule. Copies are usually available to those who attend, and your school has the right to copies of the minutes. If the minutes are prepared carefully, communication between you and the board will be enhanced. This communication will enable you to better understand the goals of your board, and will keep you informed of new rules or regulations that affect your employment.

The agenda is seldom deviated from. A good agenda will follow regular parliamentary procedure. This allows old business to be taken care of and also allows for public questions and comments on issues of concern at the present time. The meetings must be convened properly, and with a proper quorum. If this is not done, the board's actions have no effect. Individual members have no legal power—the power lies with the board as a whole.

At times, closed meetings, often called executive sessions, might be called. Even though there may be a majority of the members present, actions taken in this session have no legal effect unless and until they are made open to the public, discussed at a public meeting, and then formally decided. The private meeting is usually held to discuss acquisition of property, or special problems within the district. Some problems can best be handled privately, when they are not matters of immediate public concern. If there is some type of clash between members of the board, or with personnel, they are ironed out, if possible, in this meeting. "However, a careful distinction should be drawn between personality conflicts and philosophical conflicts or differences of opinion, since these should be discussed in open board meetings."[6] Hearings on dismissal or non-renewal of your contract may be closed to the public, if you so desire.

Closed meetings of the board are not popular with the public, so they are kept at a minimum. Where they are called, those outside of the meeting do not necessarily have a right to know what transpires. The topics discussed, and the solutions made, are not matters of public record.

SCHOOL BOARD POLICIES, POWERS AND DUTIES

As previously stated, it is the duty of the board to define its educational policies, not to implement them. There are times when it is difficult to distinguish between these two duties. The school board makes policy decisions which you will no doubt look at when you make your decision as to whether or not you want to work in that district. School board policy is a clear, concise statement of the goals the board wishes to obtain and the method in which these goals are to be accomplished. Objectives of the board are clearly defined, and guidelines should be given as to how these objectives will be realized. The guidelines are not necessarily rules and regulations, but are *broad* procedures indicating courses of action for various circumstances that will or are expected to arise. Policies, then, give direction, but the exact steps to be taken are left to school administrations.

School boards may also adopt basic rules and regulations. However, these rules and regulations are again for the purpose of giving direction to adopted policies. They are not exact rules and regulations covering every detailed step in the daily administration of the schools. The rules and regulations of the board put the policy into practice. The rules and regulations of your administration govern the daily operations of this practice.

It should be remembered that the rules and regulations of your local board must be:

1. Reasonable,
2. Pursuant to proper procedures, and
3. Within the powers granted by the state.

> If regulations are attacked for failure to meet these tests, the courts can measure the regulations by the tests to qualify the regulations as being valid or invalid.[7]

Your local school board has the final authority in deciding its educational policies. This authority is not absolute, however. The local board must also consider the state board of education, and laws governing local policies. For example, in one case, parents tried to prevent sex and family education courses from being required. The Maryland state board of education said that such courses were necessary, and the court said that the local board had the responsibility of carrying out this requirement.[8]

We all know that there will be times when the rules and regulations of the board will lean towards implementation of policy rather than direction of policy. This overlap may be all right so long as there is a clear statement of the board's intent, and so long as the rules and regulations do not substantially interfere with the initiation of policy by the superintendent. Problems may occur in this area, and they can be avoided if the board follows proper guidelines in determining its policies.

First of all, policies should be set down in writing. This writing should be a comprehensive statement of the district's objectives, and should be kept up to date. If your board does this, decisions will be consistent with one another, and claims of unfairness will be avoided. The written policies should develop from past experiences, and should involve the ultimate objectives of the community and the teaching staff as a whole. If this is the case, all persons involved will have a better understanding and trust in the objectives as stated.

School board policies should:

1. Be the result of a community effort, and fit the needs unique to each district;
2. Be flexible and open to revision;
3. Be easy to locate and use;
4. Be clear, concise, and yet comprehensive of foreseeable issues or problems;
5. Distinguish between policies, rules and regulations.[9]

The policies of your local board deal with a great many matters. Among these matters should be:

1. Regulations for board meetings and guidelines for community involvement;
2. Stated policies in relation to school personnel, including statements on teachers' duties, contract rights and responsibilities, curriculum requirements, evaluation procedures and grievance procedures;
3. Stated policies in relation to students, including statements on student conduct requirements, attendance, extra-curricular activities, and grievance procedures;
4. Stated policies in relation to school property, including statements on special services offered, such as nursing and lunch programs, maintenance of school grounds, and equipment and finance procedures.

Written policies generally contain many collateral matters within these subsections. All of these matters help to define the goals of the school board, and a thorough knowledge of the policies will help you to understand the framework within which you work. Written policies constitute a major task of the board. If this task is accomplished fairly and properly, your task will be easier to accomplish, and your students will benefit accordingly.

HOW DOES THE SUPERINTENDENT FUNCTION
BETWEEN THE BOARD AND HIS STAFF

One of the most important decisions a school board must make is its choice for a superintendent of schools. The school superintendent must be able to work with the community, the board, and with his administrative staff. The job entails a great many duties and responsibilities, and the superintendent must sort out conflicting philosophies and reach compromises that tend to satisfy all groups, while benefiting the students as a whole.

As chief executive officer of the board, it is the superintendent's responsibility to carry out the board's policies and objectives. The superintendent is the board's chief advisor on all problems concerning the district, and the board acts through the superintendent in the administration of personnel and curriculum matters. This means that the superintendent must be well informed about school procedures, he should have a sound educational philosophy that compliments the policies of the board, and he must be knowledgeable about new educational trends and improvements. His job is extremely important, in that if the superintendent performs his function properly, the district which he supervises will run smoothly towards accomplishing its educational objectives.

The superintendent's first loyalty should be to students, and he must consider what is best for them. Taxpayers, board members and teachers also consider students. However, there might be differences of opinion as to what is paramount in the line of necessities, be it salaries and curriculum or facilities and finances. The superintendent must take these opinions into consideration and give recommendations to the board. The board weighs the superintendent's suggestions, and then makes a decision. As one can easily see, the superintendent is in a tenuous position, and is sometimes pulled from three different directions. Therefore, he should have his role defined clearly, and there should be a careful distinction made between the board's responsibility and the superintendent's authority.

Like the board, the superintendent should *not* be directly involved in the teaching process by trying to control a teacher's behavior or teaching methods. This function is better left to teachers and to one's immediate supervisor who is in a better position to evaluate the teacher's effectiveness. Nevertheless, the superintendent must consider the day-to-day operations of the school district and the classroom. This means that the superintendent is concerned with the implementation of board policies, but a teacher is generally free to achieve the board's goals in his own way. Teachers are expected to be mature in all respects, but they are not restricted to narrow directions and procedures. In other words, a teacher is free to stimulate his students, and also free from unwarranted criticisms. All this is possible when the superintendent stays within the scope of his authority.

The scope of the superintendent's authority can be defined. He is the main link between teachers and the board. His duties and responsibilities include:

1. Day-to-day guidance over school policies and operations;
2. Writing clear and complete evaluation reports as to the progress or lack of progress of the board's goals;
3. Investigating questions of competency, or issues of a controversial nature;
4. Making a report, and giving recommendations, as a result of his investigation;
5. Suggesting policies that should be implemented, and giving evidence to support his suggestions;
6. Evaluating teachers' performance through his administrative staff, including principals, vice-principals and heads of departments;
7. Giving accurate and complete information on all issues and operations of the school;
8. Interviewing and evaluating teacher applicants, and giving recommendations as to who should be hired or retained;
9. Attending all board meetings, and voicing his opinion on all issues except his salary.

The superintendent performs a very necessary function in education. He reports to the board and makes suggestions as to what needs are to be considered and acted upon. He is the main administrator and his recommendations are generally given serious consideration. These decisions affect your responsibilities, and you should therefore make known your desires and support your superintendent's actions. He is your main voice to the board, and he is a strong influence in securing community and board support for your goals with students.

As you can see, the superintendent has many powers and responsibilities, but there are also basic limitations to his authority as a representative of the school board. Although the school board has the right to manage the schools, and is the teachers' employer, the board is not supposed to be involved in every aspect of education. How can one resolve the board's desire to be involved in every aspect of education, and the teacher's interest in preserving his own methods and educational commitments? What should be realized at the outset is the fact that teachers are generally in the best position to know and to understand the necessities of individual students. Teachers are trained to perform the function of transmitting knowledge and, therefore, they should be free to perform these duties without narrow restrictions. Boards, at the same time, are imputed with the duty of running the school system as a whole. If teachers and school boards objectively perform their particular tasks, and if the superintendent works as a link between these groups, communication will be enhanced, and students will obtain a better education as a result.

GETTING TEACHERS AND STUDENTS INVOLVED

The main concern of all those in education should be student achievement. We can divide those concerned into four groups: people in the community, administrative staff of the school district, professional staff, and students. Without any of these groups, the school as we know it could not exist. This fact should point out the necessity of having each group represented in the decision making process. The idea is not new. More and more school boards are listening to the opinions of all people concerned. This trend should continue, and it will, with a positive attitude of working together for the betterment of education.

The school board is made up of people in the community. The administrative staff, through the superintendent, has an important voice in board meetings; but teachers and students have no direct representation. It seems logical, therefore, that representatives of these groups should be involved at meetings of the board.

Teachers are assigned to a classroom with a job to do. They are given a great deal of professional responsibility, they are called professionals, and yet they are not given much professional authority. This could be remedied through a better understanding between the groups involved. Teachers should talk with their boards and develop a situation whereby a teacher representative is allowed to perform as a quasi-member at all board meetings. If this were done, problems and issues of concern could be better defined and handled. Furthermore, board members should be invited to teacher meetings. The board member would be able to voice his opinion on topics discussed and communicate those matters which are of concern to the board.

Through teacher involvement in school board meetings, the board would be able to utilize the knowledge and professional expertise of the people who really are aware of the needs and desires of students. Idealistically, teachers' ideas would be utilized in the formation of policies involving:

1. Textbook adoptions;
2. Curriculum planning;
3. Lesson plans, supplementary materials, and teaching methods;

4. Rules and regulations governing teacher and student conduct;
5. Recruitment of colleagues and promotions; and
6. General working conditions and facility planning.

Student participation in major issues of concern has also increased tremendously from the past. Student criticism and activism has resulted in many constructive and valuable changes. With the recognition of student rights comes an expansion of the student's role within the educational system. This points out a strong need for listening to student concerns and respecting student opinion. For example, in Santa Barbara, California, the local board of education recognizes a high school board of education. The student board meets the day before the regular board meeting and follows the procedures of the regular board. The student board makes reports and gives recommendations the following evening. The student report is a part of the regular agenda, and the idea is a large step forward in assuring a smooth running district represented by all groups involved with the education of children.

SCHOOL BOARD DISCRETION AND THE COURTS

School boards have discretionary powers granted to them by state legislatures. The local boards then exercise these powers in the best way they can. Nevertheless, mistakes are made by even the best boards of education, and sometimes their decisions need to be examined by the courts.

In the past, the courts seldom ventured into the realm of board decisions in order to determine if the board acted properly. This has changed to some degree, and the courts will review board decisions in proper circumstances. It is appropriate for the courts to review whether or not the board has performed its discretionary powers properly. However, there are guidelines that the courts tend to follow.

The local board sets its policies and standards for the district. The law has been that: "Unless the standards are so irrelevant and inappropriate as to be palpably arbitrary and unreasonable, the court must sustain them...."[10] In other words, a court, when it hears a case, will examine the circumstances which prompted the decision of the board. Where there is evidence to support that decision, the court will rule in the board's favor. However, "[d]iscretion means the exercise of judgment, not bias or capriciousness."[11] This means that the evidence supporting the board's decision must be substantial enough to withstand objective analysis by the court. Where the decision does not withstand the analysis, the board's decision will be reversed

GUIDE RULE

"SOME" EVIDENCE IS NOT ENOUGH. WHEN THE BOARD MAKES A DISCRETIONARY DECISION, IT MUST PROVE BY COMPETENT EVIDENCE THAT IT ACTED PROPERLY, AND THAT ITS DECISION HAD A SUBSTANTIAL RELATIONSHIP TO THE WELFARE OF THE BOARD.

Welfare of students is the main concern of all those involved with education. However, as you can see, this concern must be voiced by following the proper channels. The channels are defined by the rules and regulations of state boards of education and by the courts. Local boards are given guidelines to follow, and the local boards, in turn, set up guidelines for educational goals and policies that teachers are expected to pursue.

The policies of the board should be written, and should consist of clear, concise statements of educational objectives and methods of accomplishing such goals. Rules and regulations must be reasonable, pursuant to proper procedure, and within the powers granted by the state. Once the policies and rules and regulations have been stated, they should be implemented by the superintendent. If boards, administrations and teachers each perform their functions properly, and with communication between each of these groups, educational standards will be augmented and students will benefit as a result.

FOOTNOTES

1 "What Every School Board Member Should Know," New Jersey State Federation of District Boards of Education, Trenton, N.J., p.7, 4th ed. (1969).

2 *Handbook for School Board Members,* Preliminary Draft, Revised 1969 ed., Oregon School Boards Assn., University of Oregon, Eugene, Ore., p.2 (1969).

3 *Ibid.*

4 "Guide For School Board Members in Oregon," published by the Oregon School Board's Association, University of Oregon, Eugene, Ore., p.5 (1962).

5 "What Every School Board Member Should Know," New Jersey State Federation of District Boards of Education, Trenton, N.J., p.12, 4th ed. (1969).

6 *Handbook for School Board Members,* Preliminary Draft, Revised 1969 ed., Oregon School Boards Assn., University of Oregon, Eugene, Ore., p.6 (1969).

7 Kentucky State Board of Business Schools v. Electronic C.P.I., Inc., 453 S.W.2d 534, 536 (Ky. 1970).

8 Cornwell v. State Bd. of Ed., 428 F.2d 471 (4th Cir., Maryland 1970).

9 *How to Develop Written Board Policies,* N.S.B.A.–N.E.A. Joint Committee, 1960 NSBA, Inc. and NEA.

10 Anonymous v. Board of Examiners of Bd. of Ed., 318 N.Y.S.2d 163, 166 (Sup. Ct., Sp.T., N.Y. 1970).

11 Johnson v. Branch, 364 F.2d 177, 181 (4th Cir., N.C. 1966).

NINE

Recognizing Student Rights

A juvenile was sent to the state reform school for a period of up to six years. He had been found guilty of making an obscene phone call to a neighbor. Had he been an adult, the maximum punishment could have been a $50 fine and two months in jail. The United States Supreme Court overruled the guilty verdict and said that, where a substantial penalty is involved, a juvenile, like an adult, is entitled to due process of law. This case established, for the first time, that the Bill of Rights is not for adults alone; juveniles have rights, too.[1]

As a result of this decision, a landslide of cases involving infringement of student rights befell the courts. Cases involving dress codes, underground newspapers, and demonstrations, among others, were decided. In many cases, the students alleged infringement on their constitutional right of free speech, freedom of the press, freedom of assembly, equal protection, due process and privacy.

Whether or not students had rights while they were in school had never before clearly been established. The traditional judicial attitude was expressed in a case upholding a regulation requiring student attendance at weekly chapel services:

> By voluntarily entering the university, or being placed there by those having the right to control him, he necessarily surrenders very many of his individual rights. How his time shall be occupied, what his habits shall be, his general deportment ... his hours of study and recreation—in all these matters, and many others, he must yield obedience to those who for the time being are his masters.[2]

In view of the Supreme Court's 1967 decision, this traditional view that educational privilege could be conditioned on the surrender of constitutional rights no longer seemed to be supported; and in 1968, the Supreme Court, for the first time in 25 years, agreed to review a case which questioned whether or not students had a right to free speech. It ruled that:

> First Amendment rights, applied in light of the special characteristics of the school environment, are available to teachers and students. It can hardly be argued that either students or teachers shed their constitutional rights to freedom of speech or expression at the schoolhouse gate.[3]

Many school district personnel found themselves unprepared to meet a challenge to their authority. Their rules for student conduct and discipline had seldom, if ever, been questioned. They still had the power to make such rules, but now, if those rules infringed on the students' rights, they could be justified only if they were reasonable. Therefore, as the law now exists:

> Courts are reluctant to interfere with the relationship existing between student and administrator within the school system unless conflicts arise which "directly and sharply implicate basic constitutional values". . . . However, it is also clear that students do not leave fundamental rights on the school doorstep as they enter. . . . Therefore, when the state, acting through its public schools, abridges or limits a right guaranteed to the individual by the Constitution, it bears a substantial burden of justification.[4]

There is a need for school officials to prescribe and control conduct in the schools. There is a need to preserve the peace and harmony; therefore, action may be taken. But First Amendment freedoms need breathing space to survive; as a result, rules and regulations must be narrowly drawn, so as to protect the essential areas without broadly curtailing the students' rights.

Schools must serve as exemplars of respect for individuals. Respect underlies trust. In order for the teacher-student relationship to survive, attention must be given to the problems involving student rights and responsibilities. In the past, schools were unprepared to meet the challenge of youthful unrest. Today, teachers appreciate the necessity of recognizing individual's rights. Administrators, teachers and students working together can safeguard everyone's rights. You can expect and demand student support; for as one writer states:

> . . . [S]tudents bear a general responsibility to support the institution's effort to maintain a spirit of free inquiry and respect for the rights of others. This responsibility arises from the fact that students are the present beneficiaries of that traditional spirit, and are best positioned to preserve, improve, and transmit it to future generations. This responsibility imposes a duty on students not only to refrain from conduct which obstructs such effort of the institution, but also to support the enforcement of institutional discipline

designed to deter or prevent such conduct and the enforcement of civil laws where such enforcement is reasonably deemed by responsible officials to be necessary to the continued operation of the institution.[5]

A new emphasis on reaction and attitude has emerged in the schools. The school is no longer merely a tool for the transmission of ideas, but has changed to a system where children learn through experience and contact with each other and their teachers. Schools are giving way to creativity, commitment and concern for public issues. As students become involved with the ideas and activism of the times, school boards, administrators, and teachers are confronted with an increased number of new legal problems. Their response will either ensure the students of their constitutional rights—or will treat students as second-class citizens. You have taught students what the Constitution and our system of democracy means. By realizing the extent and nature of student rights, and the countervailing interests of the school, you can help to assure students that the Rule of Law which you have taught them will not be denied to them.

STUDENTS' RIGHTS TO FREEDOM OF SPEECH

Symbolic Speech:

In the late 1960's, several high school and junior high school students, with the encouragement of their parents and other adults, planned to express their opposition to American involvement in Vietnam by wearing black armbands to school. School officials learned of the plan and enacted a new regulation prohibiting the wearing of armbands on school property. The new rule was announced at a school assembly, and it was announced that refusal to remove such armbands would result in suspension. Several students wore black armbands to school, refused to remove them, and were suspended. The Supreme Court of the United States, however, enjoined the school officials from disciplining the children, saying that First Amendment rights are available to students. The Court went on to say that the state may regulate the school's curriculum, but:

> School officials do not possess absolute authority over their students. Students in school as well as out of school are "persons" under our Constitution. They are possessed of fundamental rights which the State must respect.... In our system, students may not be regarded as closed-circuit recipients of only that which the State chooses to communicate. They may not be confined to the expression of those sentiments that are officially approved. In the absence of a specific showing of constitutionally valid

reasons to regulate their speech, students are entitled to freedom of expression of their views.[6]

This right of free expression is not absolute, however. School officials must be free to prescribe and control conduct, in order to preserve the peace, harmony and efficient operation of the schools. Therefore, the Supreme Court established the rule that:

GUIDE
RULE
THE STUDENT'S RIGHT TO FREE SPEECH MAY BE RESTRICTED ONLY WHERE IT CAN BE DEMONSTRATED THAT THE ACTIVITY "MATERIALLY AND SUBSTANTIALLY INTERFERE(S) WITH THE REQUIREMENTS OF APPROPRIATE DISCIPLINE IN THE OPERATION OF THE SCHOOL."

This means that students have a guaranteed right to free expression, so long as the orderly process of education is not impaired. Emphasis in the armband case was placed on the fact that no disturbances or disorders occurred. The responsibility for maintaining peaceful expression without disrupting the educational process is placed where it belongs—on students themselves.

"Material and substantial interference" involves more than a mere desire to avoid discomfort. The Supreme Court says that some minor disruption and discomfort is to be expected, but it must be tolerated because free speech invites dispute. It often strikes at prejudices and preconceptions, and has an unsettling effect as it seeks acceptance of an idea. As stated by Justice Brandeis in 1927, a "reasonable" ground must be shown to curtail freedom of expression:

> Fear of serious injury cannot alone justify suppression of free speech and assembly. Men feared witches and burnt women. It is the function of speech to free men from the bondage of irrational fears. To justify suppression of free speech there must be reasonable ground to fear that serious evil will result if free speech is practiced. There must be reasonable ground to believe that the danger apprehended is imminent.[7]

The "material and substantial disruption" test was adopted from a case which involved students wearing freedom buttons. School officials enacted a rule which prohibited students from wearing "SNCC" (Student Non-Violent Coordinating Committee) and "One Man One Vote" buttons on school grounds. School officials argued that such a regulation was permissible because it was possible that, if students were allowed to wear the buttons, other students would ask about them, thereby disrupting the order of the classroom. The court ruled that mere apprehension of such interference, without any actual facts substantially supporting a reasonable forecasting of disruption, could not justify the regulation.[8] However, where actual disruption occurs, the students may be suspended for refusing to remove the buttons.[9]

As a result of these cases, the following rules have evolved:

GUIDE RULE

1. DISCUSSION AND EXPRESSION OF ALL VIEWS RELEVANT TO THE SUBJECT MATTER IS PERMITTED IN THE CLASSROOM, SUBJECT ONLY TO YOUR RESPONSIBILITY TO MAINTAIN ORDER.
2. WHILE THE MINIMAL DISTRACTION OF SYMBOLIC SPEECH IS TO BE ALLOWED, THE EQUIVALENT SPOKEN IDEA IN THE MIDDLE OF AN UNRELATED CLASS DISCUSSION NEED NOT BE TOLERATED.
3. BUTTONS, ARMBANDS AND OTHER SYMBOLIC SPEECH ARE NOT PERMISSIBLE IF THE MESSAGE IS SUCH AS MOCKS, RIDICULES OR IS INTENDED TO DISRUPT THE EDUCATIONAL PROCESS BECAUSE OF RACE, RELIGION OR NATIONAL ORIGIN.
4. DISTRIBUTION OF BUTTONS, ARMBANDS, ETC., IN HALLS OR CLASSROOMS DURING CLASS MAY BE PROHIBITED.

These rules help protect the students' rights, and they also help you. It is appropriate that young minds grapple with public issues and a public school is a good place to do so. Some disagreement can be anticipated, but as teachers, you realize the value of such disagreement; it shows that the students are thinking and responding. You work at challenging the students so that what you say will not be received passively, without care or thought. If you are to successfully encourage students to think and learn on their own, you and your administrations must help to safeguard the students' rights to speak freely.

In addition to the right to free expression in the classroom, the students have a right to free speech throughout the campus. The reasons for allowing such a right were stated by the Supreme Court:

The principal use to which the schools are dedicated is to accommodate students during prescribed hours for the purpose of certain types of activities. Among those activities is personal intercommunication among the students. This is not only an inevitable part of the process of attending school; it is also an important part of the educational process. A student's rights, therefore, do not embrace merely the classroom hours.

**GUIDE
RULE**

WHEN HE IS IN THE CAFETERIA, OR ON THE PLAYING FIELD, OR ON THE CAMPUS DURING THE AUTHORIZED HOURS, HE MAY EXPRESS HIS OPINIONS, EVEN ON CONTROVERSIAL SUBJECTS LIKE THE CONFLICT IN VIETNAM, IF HE DOES SO WITHOUT "MATERIALLY AND SUBSTANTIALLY INTERFERING WITH THE REQUIREMENTS OF APPROPRIATE DISCIPLINE IN THE OPERATION OF THE SCHOOL" AND WITHOUT COLLIDING WITH THE RIGHTS OF OTHERS.[10]

Although the courts have yet to distinguish, it is possible that different standards for expression of opinion in the classroom and on school premises exist. More of an imminent danger would seem to be needed where the activity is merely on school premises. Also, since younger students are more easily distracted, it would seem reasonable to assume that the regulations on speech at the elementary level could be more restrictive.

There are many ways of expressing opinion. Student expression outside the classroom has taken many forms, including demonstrations and picketing, school newspapers, underground newspapers, and personal appearance. These activities present varied legal problems.

Demonstrations:

Sit-ins, student demonstrations, picketing and civil disobedience have brought the courts many cases to consider on "idea/action" as speech. Such action has not reached public schools to the extent it has reached college campuses, but there is evidence that it is only a matter of time.[11] As campus activism becomes more common, school officials should formulate rules which confront the problem without violating the students' rights.

In 1966, a group of black students seeking integration of the faculty conducted a library sit-in. The United States Supreme Court said:

> ... [T]hese rights [free speech and assembly] are not confined to verbal expression. They embrace appropriate types of action which certainly include the right in a peaceable and orderly manner to protest by silent and reproachful presence, in a place where the protestant has every right to be ....[12]

Since such a right is recognized, it cannot be unreasonably infringed upon. It is unreasonable for schools to have a complete ban on all demonstrations. Students have a right to present their grievances before the school; therefore, requiring prior administrative approval for all "parades, celebrations and demonstrations" has been held to be an unconstitutional restraint on students' First Amendment rights.[13] This means that:

GUIDE PEACEFUL DEMONSTRATIONS CANNOT BE TOTALLY PRO-
RULE HIBITED WITHIN SCHOOL PREMISES.

There is no unlimited right to demonstrate, however. School authorities have an obligation to protect against disruption of the school and to protect other students from harassment or coercion. As a result, more disruptive activities, such as marching and picketing, may be partially restricted, but must be allowed if they take place on a portion of the school grounds and at a time when they are not disruptive. This suggests that regulations on the time, place or manner of speech may be reasonable rules. They are a condition of speech rather than a limitation of the freedom. Such rules may be used if they are necessary to protect the safety or rights of the other students, or to protect the property and normal operations of the school. This means that:

GUIDE
RULE

1. STUDENTS HAVE THE RIGHT TO ASSEMBLE PEACEABLY IN SCHOOL BUILDINGS, BUT THEY HAVE NO RIGHT TO EXCLUDE OR DISRUPT OTHERS FROM FREE MOVEMENT IN THE AREA OR BUILDING.
2. STUDENTS MAY NOT ENGAGE IN DESTRUCTION OF PROPERTY, RIOTOUS ACTION OR OTHER UNLAWFUL ACTS AND EXPECT PROTECTION THROUGH THE FIRST AMENDMENT.
3. IF THE DEMONSTRATION DEPRIVES OTHERS OF THE RIGHT TO PURSUE THEIR STUDIES IN A RELATIVELY TRANQUIL ATMOSPHERE, IT MAY BE RESTRICTED.
4. EVERY STUDENT HAS THE RIGHT TO BE INTERVIEWED ON CAMPUS BY RECRUITERS FOR MEMBERSHIP IN LEGAL ORGANIZATIONS, BUT ANY STUDENT OR GROUP MAY PROTEST AGAINST THE ORGANIZATION IF HE DOES NOT INTERFERE WITH THE OTHER STUDENTS' RIGHT TO HAVE SUCH AN INTERVIEW.

Speaker Bans:

If your school system opens a forum for free expression of ideas, it cannot exceed constitutional limitations in picking the ideas it wishes to be freely expressed. Courts are reluctant to uphold speaker bans because such bans normally result in discrimination against minority viewpoints. Prohibitions based solely on the reputation or credentials of the speaker are not justifiable. Although schools rightfully desire to shield students from "dangerous" or "immoral" forms of speech, the ban should be on the subject matter of the speech—not on the speaker. In other words, a requirement that the speech must relate to a subject of scholarly or intellectual inquiry is a reasonable rule. Nevertheless, this kind of rule is difficult to administer and is subject to abuse.

School Publications:

For many years, school newspapers have been prevalent in schools, and many schools have also encouraged the publication of student literary magazines. You may be asked to serve as an advisor for student publications, and you should be aware of what your function will be, as well as what students are allowed to print.

A 1970 case helps to point out the importance of realizing what can be printed in the school newspaper. In this case, a school board was held to be entitled to consider the contents of a school newspaper and the teacher's responsibility as advisor for the newspaper.[14] One of the newspaper's stories, entitled the "Meany Master," sharply attacked a member of the high school faculty. The newspaper also included a picture of a row of urinals, which was considered by the school board to be offensive and out of place. The court stressed that the speech was not of a controversial subject but was in the nature of a personal attack. The court said the teacher had a duty to prevent such printings, and was incompetent by failing to do so. If the items had been in the nature of constructive criticism, or of a controversial topic, the students would have had a right to print them, and the teacher would not have been responsible.

GUIDE RULE THE SCHOOL BOARD MAY CONSIDER THE CONTENTS OF A SCHOOL NEWSPAPER AND THE TEACHER'S RESPONSIBILITY AS ITS ADVISOR. ATTACKS BASED ON PERSONAL, ETHNIC, RELIGIOUS OR RACIAL BIAS SHOULD NOT BE ALLOWED TO BE PUBLISHED IN SCHOOL NEWSPAPERS.

The American Civil Liberties Union published a pamphlet which sets out guidelines for student rights.[15] As for student publications, it suggests:

> The preparation and publication of newspapers and magazines is an exercise in freedom of the press. Generally speaking, students should be permitted and encouraged to join together to produce such publications as they wish. Faculty advisors should serve as consultants on style, grammar,

format, and suitability of the materials. Neither the faculty advisors nor the principal should prohibit the publication or distribution of material, except when such publication or distribution would clearly and imminently threaten to disrupt the educational process, or might be of a libelous nature. Such judgment, however, should never be exercised because of disapproval or disagreement with the article in question.

. . . .

The freedom to express one's opinion goes hand in hand with the responsibility for the published statement. The onus of decision as to the content of a publication should be placed clearly on the student editorial board of the particular publication. The editors should be encouraged through practice to learn to judge literary value, newsworthiness, and propriety.

The right to offer copies of their work to fellow students should be accorded equally to those who have received school aid, and to those whose publications have relied on their own resources.[16]

Student newspapers can be valuable as a learning process for administrators as well as students. A showing of what students are thinking, and valid, constructive criticism can help to improve administrations and the educational system. As a group of educators stated:

Student publications and the student press are a valuable aid in establishing and maintaining an atmosphere of free and responsible discussion and of intellectual exploration on the campus. They are a means of bringing the students' concerns to the attention of the faculty and the institutional authorities and of formulating student opinion on various issues on the campus and in the world at large.[17]

Student publications can be two-sided: on the one hand, it is often feared that criticism of school officials and personnel may undermine student confidence in them, and therefore affect the quality of instruction, proper order, and discipline. On the other hand, students are acutely aware of the issues affecting their school life, and responsible criticism by them can be quite valuable and perform an important function. The task becomes one of balancing the two sides. A look at several of the cases which have arisen will help to demonstrate what some of the problems are, and how the courts will decide them.

In one case, in the late 1960's, several students sought to buy advertisement space in their school newspaper in order to express their opposition to the war in Vietnam. School officials refused them the space, but a Federal District Court ruled that such action was unconstitutional.[18] The court said that within the context of the school and the educational environment, the newspaper was a forum for dissemination of ideas. It was unfair, in light of free speech, to close to students the forum they deemed effective to present their ideas. The commitment of administrators to publish was held to also be an obligation to respect students' freedom of expression. Thus, freedom of expression in officially sanctioned newspapers is a protected right.

Legitimate criticism of state officials in a sanctioned newspaper is also entitled to the protections provided by the First Amendment. Such was the holding of a case in which a student had written, but was warned not to publish, an editorial criticizing the Governor of Alabama and the Alabama legislature for their views on student-invited speakers.[19] He was wrongfully suspended, the court said, for putting the word "censored" where his editorial would have been.

The lesson to be gained from these cases is that:

GUIDE **RULE**	WHERE THE SCHOOL HAS OPENED THE NEWSPAPER AS A FORUM FOR THE DISSEMINATION OF STUDENT IDEAS, BROAD CENSORSHIP OF EDITORIAL POLICY IS NOT WARRANTED. LIMITED REVIEW IS PERMISSIBLE, BUT THE STUDENTS HAVE A RIGHT TO EXPRESS THEIR CRITICISMS OR IDEAS WHEN SUCH EXPRESSION WILL NOT CLEARLY MATERIALLY AND SUBSTANTIALLY AFFECT THE DISCIPLINE AND OPERATION OF THE SCHOOL.

Underground Newspapers:

The term "underground newspapers" is meant to refer to those materials which are written and published by students at their own expense and off school premises. Such publications first received wide attention at the college level, but by the late 1960's, underground newspapers published by high school or junior high school students were prevalent in most public school systems.

Underground newspapers are usually distributed on school premises. It has been argued that newspapers are more disruptive or obtrusive than many other forms of speech, because one student must hand it to another; but in one way, it is more silent and passive—the other student has to *read* it before expression of opinion takes place. He has no choice with armbands or other symbolic speech. Also, some newspapers can be prohibited in the classroom, whereas most worn symbols of protest cannot. As a result, it can be argued that newspapers are less disruptive or threatening to classroom discipline.

Underground newspapers cover a wide range of commentary, often including attacks on school administrators and their policies. Administrators should not interfere with a student's passive expression of opinion about a controversial matter. Therefore:

GUIDE   UNDERGROUND NEWSPAPERS CANNOT BE ABSOLUTELY
RULE   BANNED OR PROHIBITED ON THE CAMPUS.

However, some of these newspapers may contain libelous, obscene or disruptive material which directly affects discipline. A look at several cases will demonstrate how the courts will treat such material, and the proper action for you to take.

In one case, an underground newspaper was distributed on campus. It berated students for apathy, called university administrators despots and problem children, and urged students to "stand up and fight" the school administration. The court said that this was not protected free speech. It was calculated to cause disturbance and disruption of school activities and to bring about ridicule and contempt for school authorities. The court added that the school administrators could easily forecast disruption and disorder, and properly acted in preventing such a result by suspending the students responsible for the publication and distribution of the newspaper.[20]

In another case, a student who had followed a pattern of gross disrespect and flagrant and defiant disobedience of school authorities was suspended when he tried to distribute an underground newspaper on school premises. The student had been warned not to distribute the paper because one of the articles called the principal "King Louis," "a big liar," and accused him of "racist views and attitudes." The court upheld the suspension, and said:

> A special note should be taken that the activities of high school students do not always fall within the same category as the conduct of college students, the former being in a much more adolescent and immature stage of life and less able to screen fact from propaganda.
> ...While there is a certain aura of sacredness attached to the First Amendment, nevertheless these First Amendment rights must be balanced against the duty and obligation of the state to educate students in an orderly and decent manner to protect the rights not of a few but of all of the students in the school system. The line of reason must be drawn somewhere in this area of ever expanding permissibility. Gross disrespect and contempt for the officials of an educational institution may be justification not only for suspension but also for expulsion of a student.[21]

Not all of the problems have such clear answers. In a 1970 case, several high school students had been expelled for writing, publishing, and distributing 60 copies of the "Grass High," an underground newspaper. The paper was published at the students' own expense, and was distributed on school premises. No commotion or disruption occurred. The paper contained 14 pages of poetry, essays, a critical editorial, and movie and record reviews. School officials objected to three parts of the essays:

(1) A suggestion that students should destroy or refuse to accept all "propaganda" that the school administration asks them to take to their parents;
(2) A criticism of school regulations, characterizing them as "utterly idiotic and asinine," and the system of education as being "dedicated to nothing but wasting time"; and
(3) An opinion that the school dean had a "sick mind."

The court ruled that the students should not have been expelled. It said that merely showing criticism of school policies is insufficient to justify suppression of speech; some disruption, interference or other additional facts are needed.[22]

Keep in mind that freedom of the press is an aspect of free speech. Even the fact that the newspaper is subsidized by the school doesn't warrant broad censorship of editorial policy, although limited review is allowed. Greater latitude must be given to student enterprises like underground newspapers.

GUIDE RULES

1. IN ALL CASES, IDEOLOGICAL CENSORSHIP MUST BE AVOIDED.
2. UNDERGROUND NEWSPAPERS MAY BE RESTRICTED AND THE RESPONSIBLE STUDENTS DISCIPLINED, IF THE PAPER IS LIBELOUS, CLEARLY OBSCENE, OR IS SUCH THAT IT WOULD REASONABLY LEAD SCHOOL OFFICIALS TO FORECAST MATERIAL OR SUBSTANTIAL DISRUPTION OF THE EDUCATIONAL PROCESS OR THE RIGHTS OF OTHERS.
3. NO PUBLICATIONS MAY BE TOTALLY PROHIBITED; BUT IN THE INTERESTS OF SAFETY, REGULATIONS MAY BE PUT ON THE TIMES AND PLACES FOR DISTRIBUTION.

The following guidelines may be of assistance in governing school publications and other materials.[23]

Guidelines for Distribution of Newspapers and Leaflets

A. *Places*

On the school sidewalk in front of the main entrance to building, and on the walk in front of the gym lobby. (In case of bad weather, two pupils only would be permitted each in the front main lobby and in the gym lobby. Specific approval to distribute materials inside would be required each time.)

B. *Time*

7:45-8:15 A.M.

2:46-3:15 P.M.

C. *Approval*

The previous day or earlier by appropriate class dean or principal, if dean should be absent. For materials not readily classifiable or approvable, more than one day should be allowed.

D. *Littering*

All distributed items which are dropped in the immediate area (on the front sidewalk and lawn to the street, for example, or the two inside lobbies and adjacent corridor for 50-75 feet) must be removed by persons distributing material. Waste baskets will be provided.

E. *Unacceptable Items*

"So called 'hate' literature which scurrilously attacks ethnic, religious and racial groups, other irresponsible publications aimed at creating hostility and violence, hardcore pornography, and similar materials are not suitable for distribution in the schools."

Materials denigrating to specific individuals in or out of the School.

Materials designed for commercial purposes—to advertise a product or service for sale or rent.

Materials which are designed to solicit funds, unless approved by the Superintendent or his assistant.

"Literature which in any manner and in any part thereof promotes, favors or opposes the candidacy of any candidate for election at any annual school election, or the adoption of any bond issue, proposal, or any public question submitted at any general, municipal or school election . . ."

F. *Acceptable Materials*

Materials not proscribed in section E unless dean or principal should be convinced that the item would materially disrupt classwork or involve substantial disorder or invasion of the rights of others.

G. *Appeal*

"Pupil denied approval may appeal to the Principal who with a student advisory committee of one representative from each class will review the matter. Should the petition be denied, the petitioner may still appeal to the Superintendent, then to the Board of Education, etc."

DRESS CODES AND APPEARANCE

The controversy over whether mini-skirts, pants suits or long hair should be allowed in the classroom appears trivial. The legal issue is serious, however. To what extent does the state have the right to regulate an individual's personal appearance?

t is settled that the school has the right to set up reasonable rules and regulations governing pupils, and this includes the power to regulate personal appearance. What is considered "reasonable" has changed over the years. Very few cases were ever decided on school dress codes. In early cases challenging such rules, courts did not wish to interfere, and held for the schools. For example, in one of the first cases, an 18-year-old high school girl was denied the right to attend school because she wore talcum powder in violation of the school rule:

> The wearing of transparent hosiery, low-necked dresses or any style of clothing tending toward immodesty in dress, or the use of face paint or cosmetics, is prohibited.[24]

The court agreed with the school board that this rule was reasonable.

Time changes people's attitude as to what is acceptable appearance; but, rather than wait for the change to take place, many students in the late 1960's turned to the courts in the hope that their new style of appearance would be viewed as a protected right. The courts did not really know what to do. Since the early cases were few in number, no precedent had been set and no clear rules had evolved. The Supreme Court of the United States had never considered a case on students' personal appearance, and it probably will continue to refuse to do so. Federal courts and state courts throughout the country were called upon to decide the issue. Since no precedent had been set, the results varied. Some courts ruled in favor of the students, and some ruled in favor of the schools.

The students argued that school dress codes infringed on their right of privacy; denied equal protection; violated due process; violated their right to free expression; and were, in general, arbitrary and unreasonable. Every possible argument was used. One case went so far as to argue that the hair rule constituted cruel and unusual punishment.[25] At first, most courts decided school dress codes were reasonable, regardless. A 1966 case received nationwide publicity. Three members of a "rock and roll" band were suspended for wearing a "Beatle type hair style," which the principal complained attracted attention and was disruptive in the classroom. The court ruled that the state's right to maintain an efficient and effective school system outweighed the students' personal and constitutional rights.[26]

A 1969 decision changed the tide in favor of the students.[27] Two high school students claimed that a student has a protected right "to present himself or herself physically to the world in the manner of his or her choice." The court agreed, and said that such a right could be impaired by the school only if there is a "compelling subordinating interest in doing so." The court rejected the school's argument that abnormal appearance is distracting, and that such students perform more poorly than "conforming" students. This case abolished the traditional presumption that the school's rule is constitutional. It imposed a burden of justification of the rule upon the schools.

In the late 1960's, federal courts heard most of the cases involving student appearance. They split about evenly on the issue. The Supreme Court had refused to hear any personal appearance cases, but in 1971, Mr. Justice Black expressed his views.[28] He suggested that the issues presented in typical appearance rule cases were too trivial to be decided by the federal courts. He said that the state courts should handle the problem. This statement appears to have had a profound effect on the federal courts, and in the future, most appearance rule cases will be heard by the state courts.

The state courts have not heard many of the cases involving student appearance. Like the federal courts, the state courts have been split on the issue. However, state courts tend to be more conservative and may be inclined toward favoring the schools. No uniform rules at the present time exist, so the validity of your school dress code will depend upon where you live.

One New York case is of particular interest. One of the state courts was called upon to decide whether or not the school board had the power to proscribe the wearing of slacks in school by female students. The court said that school board regulation of dress is valid only to the extent necessary to protect the safety of the wearer or to control disturbance or distraction which interferes with the education of other students. Therefore, regulations placed on bell-bottoms for bike riders, pants with small bells attached, or "styles which exaggerate, emphasize or call attention to anatomical details," would be permitted because they fall within the board's concerns. However, flat prohibitions against slacks are not valid, nor are regulations based on style and taste, instead of safety, order or discipline.[29]

Realizing that many courts have struck down dress codes which have no reasonable relation to educational results, most school districts have updated and liberalized their codes. Certain restrictions are reasonable in the mind of nearly all courts, and should be retained, however.

> 1. APPEARANCE MUST YIELD TO THE DEMANDS OF SAFETY. FOR EXAMPLE, THE WEARING OF LONG HAIR NEAR MACHINERY IN VOCATIONAL "SHOP" CLASSES IS NECESSARILY SUBJECT TO REGULATION.

**GUIDE
RULE**

2. APPEARANCE YIELDS TO THE REQUIREMENTS OF HEALTH. FOR EXAMPLE, IF THE STUDENT'S HAIR IS DIRTY AND INFECTED WITH LICE, HE MAY BE SENT HOME.[30]

3. APPEARANCE WHICH DOES NOT CONFORM TO THE RUDIMENTS OF DECENCY MAY BE REGULATED.

4. APPEARANCE WHICH CAUSES ACTUAL SUBSTANTIAL DISRUPTION MAY BE RESTRICTED.

Rules governing the conduct of school athletes, or their dress, hair, etc., may be different from the rules governing other students, if such rules are based on the demands of the sport or the safety of the athletes. The validity of rules going beyond such needs might be questioned.

SEARCHING STUDENTS' LOCKERS AND DESKS

The Fourth Amendment provides citizens with the right to be free from unreasonable searches and seizures. This means that no one may be subjected to serious punishment as a result of evidence obtained in such a search. Many questions have come up as to the legality of searching students' desks, lockers and persons.

The student's individual right to privacy is generally overcome by the need to protect the student body as a whole. In the interest of safeguarding your students, locker and desk inspections may be made for the purpose of finding rotten food, drugs, weapons, etc. If any contraband is found during such inspection, you have a right to confiscate it, and it may be used as evidence against the student.

Several main theories are used to support allowing searches of student lockers and desks:

1. School officials have legal custody, control and responsibility for the lockers.
2. The school stands in the shoes of the parent when the child is in school.
3. Contract theory, which mainly applies at colleges.

Although it is clear that the right to search exists, it is suggested that certain guidelines be followed, in order to prevent undesirable publicity and to help fulfill your relationship of trust to your students.

A 1970 case helps to point out how administrative searches can get out of control. In this case, the school's dean of men solicited students to provide information as to who might be in possession of marijuana. Acting upon a tip, the dean ordered a student to his office, asked him to empty his pockets, and threatened to phone the boy's father if he failed to comply. The boy finally emptied his pockets, which contained some marijuana. The search was upheld by the courts.[31] This is reasonable action by the administrator, but the dean, in this case, did much more than this. He visited weekly with the police narcotics squads, and he conducted "shake-downs," etc., of students. It is questionable whether his primary purpose in searching was to protect the health and welfare of the students, or instead, to obtain evidence for criminal convictions. Perhaps he had ceased being an educator and become an agent of the police.

In some schools, administrators force male students to empty their pockets, and female students' purses are searched.[32] One school board even suggested mandatory blood and urine tests to determine if students were using drugs.[33] School personnel want to protect against drug abuse, and rightfully so, because the school is responsible for the students' health, safety and welfare while they are on school premises. Nevertheless, as teachers, you realize that the responsibility of keeping the school free from the use of harmful drugs should be accomplished while honoring each person's individual protections and rights. You have a relationship of trust to maintain with your students, as well as a duty to report violations of the law. A guideline for administrative searches may help you to balance your students' private rights with the public need.

Suggested Guidelines

1. School lockers, desks, etc., may be inspected or searched, and prohibited material may be confiscated by the school administration.
2. Students should be informed, in advance, of the right of administrators to search lockers.
3. Students should be specifically informed of the time for locker inspection.
4. Where school officials have a *reasonable basis* for believing contraband is present, and there is a need for inspection of a given area, although no particular individual is suspected, they can and perhaps should obtain a search warrant with the aid of law enforcement officers.
5. In emergency situations, the search may be immediately instituted. No warrant or notice need be given, because of the necessity to maintain conditions of physical safety for students and teachers.
6. A written policy on locker inspections and other searches is desirable, and should be communicated to the students.

A FAIR HEARING

Traditionally, students were disciplined for fighting, cheating, stealing and profanity. Now, the schools are faced with new problems, ranging from drugs, underground newspapers and appearance, to racial conflict and demonstrations. How should disciplinary measures in these instances be handled? To a great extent, this is an administrative problem and a short, broad sketch of the requirements of what is termed "procedural due process" is all you need to know to assure yourselves and your students that you have met the requirements of fairness.

Most cases of misbehavior are handled quite easily without any formal procedure, and only those cases which involve a serious punishment like suspension or expulsion actually need be handled according to specific guidelines. In these serious cases, the rudiments of procedural due process may be required. No real formality is generally required, but some safeguards should be observed.

(1) Rules of procedure for hearings on suspension or expulsion should be prepared with the assistance of all concerned: parents, students, teachers and administrators: although only the school board has authority to adopt and promulgate the rules.

(2) The hearing procedure should be written and circulated to the students and their parents.

(3) When a possible serious breach of discipline has occurred, due process requires a right to a hearing as well as notice.

    (a) Written notice of the charges should be given to the student and his parents. The notice must be sufficient to give the student time and information to adequately prepare his side to be presented at the hearing.

    (b) The student has a right to present evidence on his behalf, to refute evidence presented against him, and generally to confront his accusers.

    (c) The student should be given the names of the witnesses against him, and an indication of the nature of their testimony.

    (d) The student has a right to refuse to offer incriminating evidence or testimony.

    (e) The student is not entitled to counsel but his parents may be present to advise their child; however, in very serious charges, an attorney may be present, although his function is limited.

    (f) The proof against the student must be clear and convincing.

    (g) A public hearing is not required.

(4) The board set up to conduct the hearing idealistically should not be made up entirely of teachers, administrators and board members. This reviewing or hearing body should be as objective and as independent of the school authorities as possible. (However, many state laws say that only the school board can expel the student.)

(5) Interim suspension may be imposed where there is reason to believe danger will be present if the student is permitted to remain in school pending a decision following a full hearing. Even so, a short, informal preliminary hearing should be held before imposing interim suspension, unless such is impossible or unreasonably difficult

(6) Discipline for minor infractions may be handled in a "summary fashion"—that is, without going through all the steps of a formal due process procedure. "Summary" also means immediate and now. The court cases infer that summary discipline may be used when the punishment is minor.

(7) The main test is one of *fairness*.

The best idea is, of course, to prevent misconduct. Rules of conduct which fit the following guidelines may be an invaluable aid in prevention.

1. Make it clear what behavior is unacceptable. Formal, elaborate rules for every possible instance of misconduct are not needed, however.
2. Standards of behavior should be in writing.
   a. Where the rule involved applies to behavior involving an aspect of freedom of speech, association, assembly or other constitutional rights, there is an obligation that the rule be stated with clarity and precision.
   b. Rules must apply equally to all students.
3. Behavior codes should be made available to students at the beginning of the year.
4. Update "old" behavior codes.
5. "Reasonableness" of rules depends in essence upon the mythical "conscience of the community." In preparing rules of conduct, idealistically, students, parents, faculty and administrators should be involved.

Behavior codes and procedures should be set up in such a way that the truth will be found, fairness will be afforded all parties, and the rules will be effective to maintain discipline and order. The scope of rules should only be sufficient to meet the needs and objectives of your school. They should not be overly broad.

MISCELLANEOUS PROBLEMS

Secret Societies:

The first Greek letter society in a secondary school was Alpha Phi, a literary society. It became a part of a fraternity in 1876. Subsequently, many secret societies patterned after college fraternities sprang up in the high schools. "Secret" as used here does not necessarily mean unknown. It is meant to refer to those "exclusive" social clubs, operated off campus, which derive membership from the students of a school. The process of selection generally is designed to compose itself of those "socially elite." There need not be any ritual or mystery about it.

Educators soon began to believe that such societies promoted cliques, engendered an undemocratic spirit of caste, and fostered contempt for school authority. Although there were redeeming values, secret societies were regulated to curb the evils.

GUIDE RULE   STUDENTS SHOULD BE FREE TO ORGANIZE AND TO PAR-TICIPATE IN GROUPS OF THEIR CHOICE, BUT THIS RIGHT IS SUBJECT TO SCHOOL RULES ASSURING THAT THE ASSOCIA-TIONS ARE NOT DISCRIMINATORY IN THEIR TREATMENT OF OTHER MEMBERS OF THE SCHOOL, NOR OPERATED IN A WAY WHICH INTERFERES WITH THE RIGHTS OF OTHERS.

Realizing this, many clubs and societies are condoned and encouraged by schools, but certain types are not. Reasonable rules are uniformly validated by the courts.

A society not open equally to all students was the subject of a California case. A member of the "Manana Club" unsuccessfully sought to have a school rule declared unconstitutional.[34] The rule stated that it was detrimental to the best interest of the school and to the discipline and morale of the students, for any pupils in the elementary, junior high or high schools to belong to any fraternity, sorority, or non-school club which perpetuates its membership by the *selection and decision of its own members.* Violation of the rule subjected pupils to suspension and expulsion. The object of the all-girls "Manana Club" was to promote among its members the reading of and acquaintance with books and poetry "in order to assist in creating an enlightened public." Even though the objectives of the group were commendable, the court felt that compliance with the rule was justifiable.

Married Students:

Early marriage has occasionally caused various problems and questions to arise. Years ago, a Mississippi school board argued that the marriage relation "brings about views of life which should not be made known to children," but the court said that marriage is "refining and elevating, rather than demoralizing," and the student must be admitted.[35] From that time on, the courts uniformly ruled that:

GUIDE RULE   STUDENTS MAY NOT BE BARRED FROM ATTENDING SCHOOL BY REASON OF MARRIAGE.

Compulsory school attendance, on the other hand, has generally been held to no longer exist upon marriage. Also, several state courts have ruled that school boards may restrict the extracurricular activities of married students, including participation in football, basketball, cheerleading and the holding of class office. School boards have argued that such restrictions are reasonable based on such factors as "Married students have new and added responsibilities, and they should devote their spare time to studying and making the marriage work."[36] As educators, you may doubt the validity of such arguments, and you may feel that such rules are discriminatory and deny married students equality in education. At the present time, most courts uphold such restrictions, but this may soon change

Pregnancy:

In 1966, a court invalidated a Texas school board rule which provided that, if a pupil "wants to start her family," she must permanently withdraw from school.[37] Although she cannot be permanently excluded, the general rule has been that a pregnant girl may be excluded for the duration of the pregnancy. There are several decisions to the contrary, however. For example, in 1971, an unwed, pregnant high school girl was reinstated to her classes. The girl presented doctors to show that her condition would not be an obstacle, and psychiatrists testified that absence from school would cause depression and mental anguish. The court summarized its decision by saying:

> ... [N]o danger to ... [the student's] physical or mental health resultant from her attending classes during regular school hours has been shown; no likelihood that her presence will cause any disruption of or interference with school activities or pose a threat of harm to others has been shown; and no valid educational or other reason to justify her segregation and to require her to receive a type of educational treatment which is not equal to that given to all others in her class has been shown.[38]

At the present time, only a minority of courts will require the school to allow pregnant students to attend classes. Nevertheless, in the best interests of your students, you can help by requesting your school to at least provide alternative facilities for pregnant students—i.e., allowing them to continue their studies at home and/or tutoring.

The plight of the student mother has concerned many educators. Some enlightened educators have demonstrated their concern by setting up special programs for married and pregnant students.[39] For example, in Azusa, California, student mothers are allowed to attend classes with their children in their regular high school. The classes provided deal with both the situation at hand and the normal academic course of study.

SUMMARY

Courts are reluctant to interfere with the relationship between students and the administrations of public schools. Where the student's rights have been abridged, however, the courts will grant aid, unless the school can justify its actions.

The Supreme Court of the United States has explicitly stated that juveniles have constitutional rights. Decisions have made it clear that students "do not shed their constitutional rights at the schoolhouse gates." The precise scope of these rights has not clearly been determined yet, but the following is the main test used to determine if restrictions on various rights are valid:

> Infringement on the student's rights is permissible only where it can be demonstrated that the activity "materially and substantially interfere(s) with the requirements of appropriate discipline in the operation of the school."

Students have a right to freedom of expression. Speech covers a wide variety of activities, including talking, symbolic speech, demonstrations, newspapers, and sometimes even personal appearance. This right of free speech is not absolute, however. The classroom is not a political forum. It is a center for study and understanding of a particular subject for which you as the teacher have professional responsibility and school accountability. Control immediately rests with you, and you have a right to keep your classroom free from distraction or disruption by students.

Students have the right to conduct peaceful demonstrations. They do not have the right to exclude others from free movement in the school, and they may not cause undue interference with the rights of others to pursue their studies. As a result, regulations on the time, place and manner of demonstrations are reasonable when they are necessary to protect the rights and safety of students and school personnel, or are necessary to protect the property and operations of the school.

Where the school has opened the newspaper as a forum for dissemination of student ideas, broad censorship of editorial policy is not warranted. Ideological censorship must always be avoided. School publications enjoy greater freedoms than they have in the past; yet not all of the questions and problems have been answered. To be safe, students must still be careful that criticism is constructive and is based on demonstrable facts in order to avoid charges of disrupting the student body and causing material interference with good order.

Underground newspapers may not be absolutely prohibited on school premises. Since safety and an educational atmosphere must be maintained, the distribution of newspapers and other material may be prohibited in the halls while classes are in session, or in areas which would be conducive to dangerous "traffic" congestion.

The law regarding students' rights to govern their own personal appearance is not well settled. Some schools and courts believe that personal appearance is often an expression of an individual's personality, heritage, race or culture, and as such is entitled to First Amendment protections. Yet, other schools and courts disagree. Nevertheless, restrictions necessary to protect the health, safety and rudiments of decency are generally upheld by all courts.

The substance of the expression is of great concern. Political protest and discussion of controversial issues are highly protected areas of speech. Protest of educational policy must be accepted unless material and substantial disruption of the educational process results. The administration's argument is that such protest should be more restricted than political protest, because it involves the internal workings of the school: curriculum, student-faculty relations, etc. The courts feel that such protest deserves the same protection, because students have a great interest in such communications, and school officials themselves may benefit from constructive criticism.

Protest of school rules is similar to and deserves the same protection as protest of school policy. It involves such things as students protesting school rules requiring "tardy slips," "absentee notes," or dress codes. Failure to comply with reasonable rules is punishable, but not the protest.

Protest often involves criticism of particular teachers or members of the administration. It is argued that such attacks cause disrespect for authority and adversely affects discipline, even though no immediate effects may be apparent. This argument cannot be sustained, because it would allow the school to prohibit all criticisms of its personnel. Students have always criticized teachers among themselves, if not publicly. Such criticisms may serve a useful, though controversial function.

School administrators may search lockers, desks or other areas where they believe rotten food, drugs, weapons or other contraband may be. A written policy on locker inspections and other searches should be drawn up and distributed to the students at the beginning of the year.

Behavior codes and procedures should be set up in such a way that the truth will be found, fairness will be afforded all parties, and the rules will be effective to maintain discipline and order. Behavior codes should be made available to students at the beginning of the year. Formal, elaborate rules are not needed for every possible instance of misconduct. Discipline for minor infractions may be handled immediately and without following any formal procedures. Where a serious penalty is involved, the student has a right to due process and therefore, a more formal due process procedure should be followed before deciding if discipline is warranted.

Students should be free to organize and participate in voluntary organizations, but these should be neither discriminatory in their treatment of other members of the school, nor operated in a way which substantially interferes with the rights of others.

Married students have a right to attend school, although compulsory attendance is generally not required. The extracurricular activities of married students may legally be restricted, but many educators disagree as to the wisdom of such restrictions. Most courts feel that pregnant students may be excluded from school for the duration of the pregnancy, but many educators are working to help provide a continuing education for such students.

Simplistic conclusions are not practical in determining the constitutional rights of students. The endless possible combinations of personalities, facts and circumstances make it impossible to definitely state the outcome of every case. If such were possible, there would be little or no need for ever taking your problems to the courts. Yet, there are benefits to be gained in realizing the extent of basic rights and responsibilities. You will know how to react to the many challenges involving the law. How teachers and administrators react to the challenge of their authority is not only important in the operations of the schools, but in the way youths will develop their attitudes toward their government. From a legal standpoint, who wins a case is not as important as why he won. From an educator's standpoint, who wins the case is not as important as why the school's disciplinary system could not have provided a solution short of having to seek help from the courts.

FOOTNOTES

1 In re Gault, 387 U.S.1 (1967).
2 North v. Board of Trustees, 27 N.E. 54, 56 (Ill. 1891).
3 Tinker v. Des Moines School District, 393 U.S. 503, 506 (1969).
4 Reichenberg v. Nelson, 310 F. Supp. 248, 251-252 (U.S.Dist. Ct. Neb. 1970).
5 _____, "A Statement of the Rights and Responsibilities of College and University Students," 1 Human Rights 140, 159 (1970), published by the Section of Individual Rights and Responsibilities of the American Bar Association.
6 Tinker v. Des Moines School District, 393 U.S. 503, 511 (1969).
7 Whitney v. California, 274 U.S. 357, 376 (1927) (concurring opinion).
8 Burnside v. Byars, 363 F.2d 744 (5th Cir. Miss. 1966).
9 Blackwell v. Issaquena, 363 F.2d 749 (5th Cir. Miss. 1966).
10 Tinker v. Des Moines School District, 393 U.S. 503, 512-513 (1969).
11 Brammer, "The Coming Revolt of High School Students," Bull. of the Nat'l Assn. of Secondary School Principals, Sept. 1968, at 13.
12 Brown v. Louisiana, 383 U.S. 131, 141-142 (1966).
13 Hammond v. South Carolina State College, 272 F. Supp. 947 (U.S. Dist. Ct. S.C. 1967).
14 Jergeson v. Board of Trustees, 476 P.2d 481 (Wyo. 1970).
15 A.C.L.U., "Academic Freedom in the Secondary Schools" (September 1968).
16 *Id.* at 11-12.
17 American Association of University Professors (1966); as reproduced in *Working Papers,* XXII Congress, U.S. Nat'l Students' Assn. (1969).
18 Zucker v. Panitz, 299 F. Supp. 102 (U.S. Dist. Ct. N.Y. 1969).
19 Dickey v. Alabama State Board of Education, 273 F. Supp. 613 (U.S. Dist. Ct. Ala. 1967).
20 Norton v. Discipline Committee of East Tenn. State University, 419 F.2d 195 (6th Cir. Tenn. 1969), cert. denied, 399 U.S. 906 (1970).
21 Schwartz v. Schuker, 298 F. Supp. 238, 242 (U.S. Dist. Ct. N.Y. 1969).
22 Scoville v. Board of Education, 425 F.2d 10 (7th Cir. Ill. 1970), cert. denied, 400 U.S. 826 (1970).
23 Guidelines resulted from the case of Goodman v. Board of Education (N.J. June 18, 1969); quoted from Nolpe Notes, vol. 6, #5, p. 1-2 (May, 1971).On March 12, 1971, the New Jersey Commissioner ruled on these guidelines and found them acceptable.
24 Pugsley v. Sellmeyer, 250 S.W. 538 (Ark. 1923).
25 Davis v. Firment, 269 F. Supp. 524 (U.S. Dist. Ct. La. 1967), aff'd per curiam, 408 F.2d 1085 (5th Cir. La. 1969).
26 Ferrell v. Dallas Independent School District, 261 F. Supp. 545 (U.S. Dist. Ct. Tex. 1966), aff'd, 392 F.2d 697 (1968), cert. denied, 393 U.S. 856 (1968).
27 Breen v. Kahl, 296 F. Supp. 702 (U.S. Dist. Ct. Wis. 1969), aff'd, 419 F.2d 1034 (7th Cir. Wis. 1969), cert. denied, 398 U.S. 937 (1970).
28 Karr v. Schmidt, 401 U.S. 1201 (Black, Cir. Justice Feb. 11, 1971), rehrg. denied, 91 S. Ct. 1248 (1971).
29 Scott v. Board of Education, Union Free School District #17, Hicksville, 305 N.Y.S.2d 601 (N.Y. 1969).
30 Carr v. Inhabitants of the Town of Dighton, 118 N.E. 525 (Mass. 1918).
31 Mercer v. State, 450 S.W.2d 715 (Tex. 1970).

32 Daniel L. Rotenberg and John W. Sayer, "Marijuana in the Houston High Schools—A First Report," 6 Houston L. Rev. 759 (1969).

33 Phyllis C. Barnes, "Drug Abuse: The Newest and Most Dangerous Challenge to School Boards," American School Bd. Jour. 18 (Oct. 1968).

34 Robinson v. Sacramento City Unified School District, 53 Cal. Rptr. 781 (Dist. Ct. App. Cal. 1966).

35 McLeod v. Colmer, 122 So. 737 (Miss. 1929).

36 Board of Directors of Independent School District of Waterloo v. Green, 147 N.W.2d 854 (Iowa 1967).

37 Alvin Independent School District v. Cooper, 404 S.W.2d 76 (Tex. 1966).

38 Ordway v. Hargraves, _____F. Supp. _____(U.S. Dist. Ct. Mass. 1971); quoted from Nolpe Notes, vol. 6, #6, p.4 (June, 1971).

39 Richard Woodbury, "Help for High School Mothers." *Life,* April 2, 1971., p. 34

Pointers for Further Reading of Legal Cases Cited in This Book

A law library is fairly complex, and is inaccessible for *research purposes* without some formal training or study. However, when you have the name and citation of a particular case, it is easy to find and read that case if you have some basic knowledge on what to look for. For additional and general information on many of the subjects covered in this book, you may also wish to refer to *Guide to School Law* and *School Law in Action: 101 Key Decisions with Guidelines for School,* both by M. Chester Nolte and published by Parker Publishing Company, West Nyack, N.Y.

There are basically three types of legal texts you will be interested in: (1) law journals or reviews, (2) state and federal statutes, and (3) books containing the complete written decision of particular cases. We feel that many of you may be interested in looking up a case which has been discussed in *The Teacher and the Law*. Generally, you should only need to know how to find a case in (3)—those texts which have the complete written decisions. Therefore, you need to know what the numbers or letters represent that follow the name of each case.

Cases are cited by (1) stating the name of the case, (2) the volume number of the book where the case is found, (3) the abbreviated name of the book, (4) the page number on which the case starts, (5) if there is a quote, the page where the quote starts and (6) in parentheses, the state from which the case arose, and the date the case was decided.

For example, the first case cited in Chapter One involved a teacher who was dismissed for his misconduct. The case is cited as Gover v. Stovall et. al., 35 S.W.2d 24, 26 (Ky. 1931).

(1) "Gover v. Stovall et. al." is the name of the case.

(2) "35" is the volume number of the book where the case is found.

(3) "S.W.2d" is the abbreviated name of the book. In this instance, the abbreviation stands for Southwestern, Second Series.

(4) "24" is the page number on which the case starts.

(5) "26" is the page on which the quote begins.

(6) "(Ky. 1931)" means that the case originated in Kentucky and was decided in 1931.

State district and circuit court cases do not generally have written decisions published. However, when a case is appealed to the higher state courts (e.g., the Court of Appeals or the state Supreme Court) written decisions are published or reported in several sets of books. Some books only cover individual state cases. Other books cover certain sections of the country. We have generally left out individual state texts and cited those books which cover various sections of the United States. In legal matters, the states are divided into geographic areas, and each area has its separate "Reporter," or, in other words, the book which reports or publishes various decisions within its area. These Reporters are called, for example, Northeastern (N.E.), Northwestern (N.W.), Southern (So.), Pacific (P.) or Atlantic (A.), and there are a few others. For most of these reporters, there are second series, and they are cited by giving the abbreviation, followed by "2d" (e.g. S.W.2d).

New York and California have an exceptionally large number of cases and since nearly all libraries have these states' reporters, we have cited these books. For our purposes, we mainly cited the New York Supplement (N.Y.S.) and the California Reporter (Cal. Rptr.).

There are several sets of books where written case decisions of the Supreme Court of the United States are reported. We have used the United States Reports and the cases are cited in this manner: 393 U.S. 503 (1969). Cases generally go to the Supreme Court by being appealed from the Federal Circuit Court, or the highest state court. When the Supreme Court refuses to review a case (denies certiorari), this is cited as: cert. denied, _____ U.S. _____ (1972).

The lowest federal court is the federal district court. Cases decided by this court can be found in a set of books called the Federal Supplement, abbreviated as F. Supp. The main difference in citations of these court decisions is that in parentheses we have added that the cases arose in the United States district court, and we name the state in which that case arose. For example: _____ v. _____, 217 F. Supp. 257 (U.S. Dist. Ct. Mass. 1967).

A federal district court case can be appealed to the federal circuit court. Case decisions from these courts are found in the Federal Reporters. The more recent cases are found in the second series of Federal Reporters, abbreviated as F.2d. The United States is divided into eleven circuits for federal court purposes, designated as first through tenth, and the District of Columbia. Therefore, in parentheses we have added the state and the circuit in which the case was decided. For example: _____ v. _____, 206 F.2d 141 (5th Cir. S. Car. 1967).

It should be easy for you to find these books and read the cases which interest you. However, if you should have any problems, show the name of the case and the citation to someone in the legal library, and he will be able to show you where the books you need can be found.

Index

McDOWELL TECHNICAL INSTITUTE LIBRARY
MARION, NORTH CAROLINA